HOUSE & GARDEN

BOOK OF STYLE

HOUSE & GARDEN

BOOK OF STYLE

BY DOMINIQUE BROWNING

SUZANNE SLESIN, CAROLINA IRVING, CYNTHIA FRANK,

ELIZABETH POCHODA, WENDY MOONAN, CAROLINE CUNNINGHAM

AND

THE STAFF OF HOUSE & GARDEN

EDITED BY JUDITH NASATIR

CLARKSON POTTER / PUBLISHERS

NEW YORK

Published by Clarkson Potter/Publishers, New York, New York.
Member of the Crown Publishing Group.
Random House, Inc. New York, Toronto, London, Sydney, Auckland
www.randomhouse.com

CLARKSON N. POTTER is a trademark and POTTER and colophon are registered
trademarks of Random House, Inc.

Printed in Hong Kong

Design by Matthew Drace/Mo Flan Industries.

Library of Congress Cataloging-in-Publication Data
House & Garden book of style; the best of contemporary decorating/ by Dominique Browning [et al.]
and the entire staff of House & Garden; edited by Judith Nasatir.
1. Interior decoration--U.S.--History--20th century. I. Title: House and Garden book of style.
II. Title: Book of style. III. Browing, Dominque. IV. Nasatir, Judith. V. House & Garden.
NK2004.H677 2001
747.213'09'04--dc21   2001032862

ISBN 0-609-60928-9
10 9 8 7 6 5 4 3 2 1
First Edition

FOREWORD

Once upon a time, there was a Kingdom of Great Style. The people who ruled it were strict about who was allowed in, and who had to be kept out; and, abiding by the rules of the One Great Decorator, they were particular indeed about how their stylish palaces were to look. Along came the new millennium. The one great kingdom wasn't banished, exactly; it simply found itself surrounded by other palaces springing up around it, one more beautiful than the last, each one heralding a new personality, a new character. The spare, elegant strength of the minimalist's regime vied for attention with the charming and colorful eccentricity of the bohemian's fiefdom. The luxurious palace filled with gorgeous antiques and sumptuous fabrics was as excellent a place to reside as the one filled with soft, comfortable armchairs in rooms that promised the repose of a countryside idyll. No one could ever agree on whose style was superior, and in fact to engage in such an argument was, finally, considered silly.

We live in a time that celebrates variety, and our job at *House & Garden* has been to chronicle all the different kinds of stylishness that enthrall and delight our modern sensibilities. The editors here are just like our readers, capable of falling in love with the gracefulness of a minimalist gem one day, and then dropping that soon after because we're swooning over the frenetic energy of an eclectic collection of treasures. Surprise, character, imagination, passion, flair, personality, integrity. That's what gives decorating its charge. That's the kind of energy that makes for great style today.

DOMINIQUE BROWNING

EDITOR-IN-CHIEF

INTRODUCTION

❧

And now, having watched the Whatnot disappear, I have the privilege of watching its resurrection. I have passed from disgust, through total forgetfulness, into the joys of retrospection.
—Roger Fry, "The Ottoman and the Whatnot," 1919

A great art critic like Roger Fry was bound to find keeping up with the style jones—identifying what's old and what's new, what's in and what's out, and especially what's next—a source of amusement. Today, fortunately, the decorating scene is less at the mercy of a passing vogue than it was in Fry's time. Choice abounds, but tradition does, too. After all, there is no such thing as spontaneous generation, especially when it comes to something as fluid as style. While what's old is transformed, inevitably, into what's new, the fundamental elements of style remain the same. They are, and will always be, form, color, line, proportion, scale, texture, pattern, and material. It's the nature of the mix that matters more than ever before.

UPDATED CLASSICS, PAGE 12

OPPOSITE: Designer Brian McCarthy and architect Boris Baranovich commissioned custom designs, including this dining room mural by Susan Huggins, to present the client's antiques collection.

NEW INTERNATIONAL,
PAGE 52

In Linda Wells's living room, John Keenen and Sills Huniford Associates created a perfect
modern environment with a muted palette and some twentieth-century design icons.

UPDATED CLASSICS

Sabots off to the Updated Classics. This style celebrates the power of the human imagination, as expressed by the human hand. Were there no tradition of decorative arts, there would be no decorating. But even those who love the past, and appreciate its comforts, exist in the here and now, where it's possible to marry the grandeur and the artisanal perfection of the eighteenth and nineteenth centuries with the practicality and technology of the twentieth and twenty-first. As designer Brian McCarthy demonstrates with the antique-filled decor for this Manhattan apartment, nothing matters more than good form, and minute attention to custom detail, except gracious living and a healthy appetite for the finer things in life.

NEW INTERNATIONAL

Behold the reinvigorated dean of twentieth-century styles. It is impossible to overestimate the impact of the International Style glass-and-steel aesthetic on the way we now live, work, and think. Modernism's rigorous approach to free-flowing space and light is headed into new territory, where an unprecedented ease and relaxed kind of rigor prevail. Today's International Style doesn't mean uncomfortable, much less unlovely. Nor does it snub the older, familiar beloved forms. The New Jersey house that architect John Keenen and interior designers Sills Huniford Associates created for Allure editor-in-chief Linda Wells and her family refines modernism to reveal its nascent hospitality to comfort and tradition.

COUNTRY LUXE

In a world that spins ever more quickly, there is no greater luxury than stopping. So celebrate the emergence of country luxe, the latest style for a getaway residence. Neither regional nor rustic, although certainly bucolic and informal, country luxe style depends on a decorating technique confident enough to relax and bring the outside inside, to remind the eye, and the inner eye, to restore itself with the pleasures of nature, family, and friends. The airy interior with a sunny palette and a collection of funky furniture that interior designer Julia Doyle has put together for a Long Island house near the beach quietly insists on just that.

MINIMALISM

For some it may be bare. For others, there may be no there there. But look again. Somewhere between the silence and the light lies Minimal Style, a pared-down approach to domestic life that solves the problem of sensory overload. Simplicity, however, does not mean plain. Or ordinary. This stripped-to-the-essence aesthetic maximizes the effect of the basic elements of style: line, plane, and volume. It brooks no interference, and it tolerates no errors in proportion or taste. Kelly Behun and Jay Sugarman's

COUNTRY LUXE,
PAGE 78
For this comfortable country house, interior designer Julia Doyle mixed funky old and new pieces and colors to match her clients' youthful spirits.

BOHEMIAN CHIC,
PAGE 134
Actor Patrick Bachau and his wife, Mijanou, filled their California house with African and Asian treasures found on location, in shops, and at auction.

weekend house in the Hamptons, like the white album that it is, captures the poetry of this particular moment in the century-long debate over whether less is more.

BOHEMIAN CHIC

Think different? Yes, those who embrace Bohemian Chic do. These are true artists of decor, and we would be duller without them. The world's determined individualists have always generated a certain respect, and not just for breaking the established rules. Today's Bohemian Chic reflects the new century's delight in people still elegantly eccentric enough to do it, find it, make it, and reveal it themselves. For example, actor Patrick Bachau and his wife, Mijanou, have filled their 1923 Los Angeles house with what most interests them. As a result, it reflects the spirit of their curious minds and their adventurous lives.

GRAND TOUR

If it's possible to know people by the company they keep, it's also possible to recognize them by the souvenirs they cherish because of the stories these objects tell. Those who live life Grand Tour-style care about stuff, but such stuff as others' dreams have realized. This style has an itinerant quality of a most particular kind, threading its way through history, circling the world, incorporating choice artifacts from eras more imperial than our own. Lars Bolander sees the world as such a stage, and the Palm Beach apartment he and his wife occupy shows it.

MID-CENTURY MODERN

Mid-century Modern style offers us a few whatnots of our own for observation. In addition to the snappy reminders of a not-so-distant past, it rides the waves of the future. How do you chart a course to reach this state of domestic grace? Couple a high regard for yesterday's talents with a taste for the sleek results of today's experiments with new materials and new technologies. This Miami residence, the sole house by the late Morris Lapidus, master of the woggle and maestro of the mosaic, shows the way. Its owners restored it to pristine condition, and filled it with postwar period pieces and Memphis icons that exemplify the passion for design.

These are heady, expressionistic times, at the onset of a new century. The variety of the world is immediate. The past, both near and distant, is at our disposal. Yet while we treasure history, we have no intention of reliving it. And while we honor tradition, we have no intention of cloning it. Style's wheel of fortune continues to turn as it did when Fry clocked it almost a century ago. But it's traveling in new directions. And so are we.

MINIMALISM,
PAGE 106
Design consultant Kelly Behun and husband, Jay Sugarman, tested their theories about living with no design in the white spaces of their weekend house in the Hamptons.

GRAND TOUR,
PAGE 162
Lars Bolander's Palm Beach apartment mixes mementos of different civilizations, including the painted copies of Roman cameos and contemporary stone urns.

MID-CENTURY MODERN,
PAGE 190

The current owners of late architect Morris Lapidus's sole private house pay homage to the master with mid-century classics by Eero Aarnio and Pierre Paulin, among others.

UPDATED CLASSICS

Appreciating the old world doesn't mean re-creating it. Here's a style where mind triumphs over matter, imagination reigns, and the fantasy is all.

Is it? Or isn't it? With traditional style there is now room for interpretation—and improvisation. Whether Regency, Empire, Art Deco, or Arts and Crafts, it's traditional if it samples elements from the decorative arts and crafts of other, often grander, times and places. As new world as it may be in its aspirations and its comforts, the traditional look itself is old world, with some or all of the following: period furniture, document fabrics, *objets de vertu,* boiserie, and passementerie.

Singularly American, this panoramic style emerged with the decorating profession itself. In *The Decoration of Houses,* their 1897 how-to classic, Boston Brahmin architect Ogden Codman and novelist Edith Wharton outlined a practical home style that equated suitability, simplicity, and comfort by declaring independence from a cluttered, claustrophobic past. The buccaneering Elsie de Wolfe, America's first decorator, formulated a recipe of chintz, boiserie, mirrors, animal-skin patterns, fine art, and eighteenth-century French and English antiques that still serves as traditional style's Rosetta stone.

Successive generations of decorators continue to reinterpret the principles of scale and proportion to suit contemporary lifestyles, to-the-manor-born fantasies, and large American dreams. Traditional stylists never forget that, in America, your home is your castle. If the dimensions aren't those of Chatsworth or Chenonceau, so be it. The constraints of accuracy need not apply, but the joyous values of exploration, discovery, expansion, splendor, grace, and the power of ornament do. Here's to illusions of grandeur and the pleasures of revisionist history.

OPPOSITE: Carved gilt Régence chairs add detail to an exuberant room by Edward Zajac and Richard Callahan.

ENGLISH HISTORY

For some decorators, the sun has never set on the British Empire. Keith Irvine of Irvine & Fleming, the New York firm known for its so very English decorating, is one of them. In his case, it's just as well. Irvine's clients, an international couple, commissioned him to design the interiors of their early-twentieth-century, double-fronted mansion on Manhattan's Upper East Side, which the designer describes as "a slightly bogus bankers' Georgian."

The house provided Irvine with a beautifully proportioned blank slate on which to develop his slightly eccentric brand of English style, one cultivated under the tutelage of John Fowler and Nancy Lancaster, two of Britain's legendary tastemakers.

Irvine's main inspiration came from the high point of the British Empire, "when the luxe building and decoration in England was phenomenal." During the last 30 years of the eighteenth century, he says, English rooms emphasized light; in the first 30 years of the nineteenth century, English rooms grew darker, but more comfortable. This 60-year period, with its contrast of styles, forms the kernel of Irvine's decor for this house.

ABOVE: A grand entrance is established with a black-and-white marble floor and sweeping stair. Much of the drama comes from Clarence House's Pembroke Damask, an overscaled hand-blocked wallpaper inspired by a seventeenth-century wallpaper at Pembroke House in England. A gilded English Regency console and rare eighteenth-century Gothic garden chairs add to an unusual mix of furnishings.
OPPOSITE: The round table is draped in Brunschwig & Fils's Harrow Damask. The carpet from Stark was custom-colored.

Throughout the house, startling color combinations and contrasting patterns occur, orchestrating a sophisticated visual counterpoint. Furniture, accessories, and lighting range from George II and eighteenth-century Gothic to Regency and William IV. Deft arrangements of pictures and bibelots enliven polished surfaces. A majestic foyer establishes the tone with a hand-plastered aqua cupola inspired by Robert Adam, the eighteenth-century neoclassical architect, a sharply patterned black-and-white marble floor, a graceful stair, and hand-blocked wallpaper. The second floor consists of an elegant enfilade of rooms for dining and sitting.

ABOVE: Paneled pine walls in the telephone room came from a house in New Hampshire. The antique English settee is covered in fabrics from Cowtan & Tout; the antique English William IV lounge chair is upholstered in Old World Weavers's Dame du Lac. **OPPOSITE:** The four shades of green strié glazes were made with one color and different degrees of brush pressure. The same effect was achieved on the moldings by brushing muslin across the wet surfaces. The red trim is plastic Letraline tape from an art supply store. The wing chairs, inspired by Nancy Lancaster's, are covered in a Brunschwig & Fils chintz. The Regency bull's-eye mirror dates to 1820.

ABOVE: In the drawing room, antique English botanical plates are artfully arranged around a 1790 Waterford mirror. The George II inlaid marble mantel dates from 1760. **OPPOSITE:** The master bedroom's elaborate canopy bed, with swooping pleats of Fancy Lining by Clarence House, a floral valance of Cowtan & Tout's Bouquet & Roses, and Stroheim & Romann's solid pink trim, is Irvine's homage to John Fowler, the founder of Colefax & Fowler, the English design house. Fowler believed in emphatically feminine master bedrooms, and, says Irvine, usually lined the inside of the bed hangings with pink fabric. The tiny settee is covered in Les Enfantes, a Clarence House toile; the club chair is in Verrières, a Brunschwig & Fils linen.

THE FRENCH
CONNECTION

In Manhattan, where even apartments have pedigrees, the 12-room residence that Linda and Gregory Fischbach acquired after a move from the West Coast harbors more than just good bones. The moderne building on Park Avenue was developed by James T. Lee, a former director of the Chase National Bank and grandfather of Jacqueline Kennedy Onassis.

Designed by Rosario Candela in association with Arthur Loomis Harmon and completed in 1929, the sleek structure was once home to Lee and, from 1932 to 1938, his daughter, Janet, son-in-law John Bouvier, and their two daughters Jackie and Lee.

Distinguished by generously proportioned rooms with marble fireplaces, lofty ceilings, and slender, brass-bound French doors that open onto three terraces, the apartment's innate spatial grace can accommodate virtually any traditional decor, and perhaps it has. One of its previous owners was Mrs. Byron C. Foy, nee Ethel Chrysler, a noted tastemaker and celebrated collector who incorporated choice eighteenth-century French elements—including the existing *parquet de Versailles* and marble floors and the boiserie in the salon and master bedroom—into a well-documented interior flush with French antiques and Impressionist paintings.

The Fischbachs prefer a more startling mix, but one that curtsies to history. While on staff at Sotheby's, Mrs. Fischbach encountered the sale catalogs for the Foy collection. She commissioned the late Mark Hampton to create an interior with an obviously French twist, "because I wanted to keep the apartment consistent with what it had once been." The Fischbachs have used their art collection—Damien Hirst, Cindy Sherman, Matthew Barney, Nan Golden, Robert Mapplethorpe, Frank Stella, Jim Dine, Roy Lichtenstein, Chuck Close, Georges Braque—to inject a bracing dose of now, with attitude, and with respect for tradition.

The salon was decorated in the spirit of Mrs. Foy, a former tenant and tastemaker, and contains the boiserie she chose when she lived in the apartment years ago.

ABOVE: The Fischbachs didn't make any major architectural changes to the interior, which consists of an L-shaped series of public rooms connected by a gallery, with living quarters behind closed doors. Three marble steps lead the way to a light-filled dining room. French doors open onto a terrace, off the home office, that often serves as a breakfast room. The gallery that connects the library to the dining room is lined with antiques and contemporary art, including a Seton Smith, a Damien Hirst, and a Stella. **OPPOSITE:** The light-blue-and-cream dining room has a Chinese motif, with delicate scenic wallpapers and a pair of lacquered screens. Mrs. Fischbach bought many of the furnishings while she was working at Sotheby's, but she found the 12 French dining room chairs in the Hamptons one afternoon on her way home from the beach.

ABOVE: The Fischbachs wanted to recapture the French spirit in the private rooms as well as the public spaces. The master bedroom still contains Mrs. Foy's original, elegantly detailed boiserie, and includes an unusual arched front that frames the fireplace, which has a mantel carved to match. The woodwork has been painted a soft, creamy yellow with white trim. The *parquet de Versailles* floor matches that of the salon. Two eighteenth-century bergères add to the French theme. **OPPOSITE:** A fresh eye with a fresh approach ensures that this classic interior will remain up to date. The marble-floored entry gallery, where one of Damien Hirst's spin paintings hangs above a graceful eighteenth-century-style settee establishes the tone with a startling combination of contemporary art and antique French furniture.

AN AMERICAN DREAM

Peter Gomes, Harvard's preacher and professor of Christian morals, is as difficult to classify as the style he has created for Sparks House, the handsome, early-nineteenth-century residence of the university's appointed man of God. As a Harvard Divinity School student, Gomes watched the house being moved from Quincy Street to its present location. During his 1974 job interview, he insisted to Harvard's president that Sparks House be part of the deal. "I don't know where I got the courage, but I rose to my full five feet four inches and said, 'But, sir, that house is as critical to the ministry, as I understand it, as a laboratory is to a chemist.'"

Gomes has reformed Sparks's dull interior with his own combination of solid Edwardian comfort and Yankee rectitude: a bracing use of color, the profligate arrangement of dissimilar things, and the mix of different histories and historical styles. His design exuberance, Gomes says, comes in part from his father, a native of the Cape Verde Islands, and in part from his mother's people, the Afro-Saxons, as he calls them, who settled in New England long ago.

As for how we are to regard the things of this world, Gomes is a firm believer that "a too spiritual religion is no earthly good." Although material things are morally neutral, as he points out in his best-seller *The Good Book: Reading the Bible with Mind and Heart*, they can become morally problematic. Still, he has no patience, he says, with "a totalitarian austerity. I don't regard that as more godly than a beautifully furnished room."

Gomes's exuberance dictates a bracing use of color, the profligate arrangement of dissimilar things, a joyful collage of different historical styles. In his study, he has rendered unto Caesar the things that are Caesar's, topping the emperor's bust with a Stetson given to him by the University of Texas. The striped chair fabric is from the English upholsterer for Windsor Castle.

ABOVE: Houses in Cambridge are known for their remarkable stairwells, and this one, flooded with light from its dome, is among the city's finest. The linen cupboard is an 1820s piece from New England. Engravings of English clerics line the stairwell. LEFT: The English hall chairs in the foyer at the base of the stairs are from the 1870s. The portrait of Mary Sparks, wife of Jared Sparks, a former president of Harvard, sits above a bachelor's table from the 1900s. OPPOSITE: The wallpaper was the idea of architect Robert Neiley. It is by Waterhouse Wallhangings, of Boston, MA, and is a copy of paper in Gunston Hall Museum, in Lorton, VA. Gomes has no patience, he says, with "a totalitarian austerity. My theology is such that I do believe that God is the author of beauty. It is not beauty that distracts us from the love of God. It is beauty that affirms the presence of God. This is not the worship of the material. This is using the gifts of God for the people of God."

ABOVE: Even the old Yankee families of Gomes's native Plymouth had a certain lushness in their lives. As a teenager, the reverend worked as a sort of houseboy, and he noticed, he says, in the rugs and mirrors, in the cabinets of Canton and Rose Medallion, a "marvelous aesthetic in the midst of the ascetic Yankee style." His study, like the rest of Sparks House, combines both tastes, the Yankee and the Anglican. The nineteenth-century American hall chair is covered in English fabric used on furniture in Windsor Castle. **OPPOSITE:** Gomes imposed his taste slowly, eventually proceeding with a full-scale overhaul that includes the living room's exuberant mix of things. He took his time, he says, because he wanted the house to be "a living, breathing thing, not a museum." He knew that if he were successful, it would help him forge a link with visiting students. "They see the exotic here, and they enter into it. There's a certain amount of fantasy in this house, and God knows these kids don't have enough fantasy."

GO FOR BAROQUE

Elaborate ornamentation provides a foundation for period styles from Baroque to English Regency to Directoire. While period agreement may be nice, an inspired mix can effortlessly transform the ordinary into the fabulous. Decorators Edward Zajac and Richard Callahan have realized just such an alchemist's dream in a 1930s Georgian-style house on Long Island belonging to merchant banker Donald Brennan and his wife, Pat, who is Callahan's sister. Fanciful draperies, lavish bed canopies, and inventive upholstery treatments impart an irrepressible spirit of charm, color, and fantasy.

"The house is a very American mixture, a collection of styles that we love, love, love," Zajac explains. "Our approach is to whip up things from years of accumulated knowledge," adds Callahan, who began his career in the New York offices of Jansen, the prestigious French firm, then joined designer Valerian Rybar. The two later spent nine years with the legendary Billy Baldwin, learning to juggle patterns and furniture styles, juxtapose colors, and layer detail upon detail without worrying about historical accuracy. "We don't like period rooms, and Billy didn't respect designers who did Louis XV or Robert Adam," Zajac asserts.

You can't improvise, though, without knowing the classics. During their student years at Parsons School of Design, the duo toured Baroque palaces in Germany, English country houses, and Venetian palazzos, all of which provided them with the sort of visual encyclopedia that every decorator needs. From the neon intensity of the foyer—inspired equally by brightly painted entrance halls in English country houses and Callahan's knowledge of his sister's taste—to the chinoiserie dining room, the decorators have filled the house with their unique confections.

ABOVE: In the study, antique English painted panels from Kentshire Galleries in New York establish an exotic tone. Brunschwig & Fils's Foret Foliage wallpaper contributes to the garden atmosphere created by the predominantly yellow and green decor. Paula Poleschner-Kucera stenciled the floor with a pattern that echoes the ottomans' tufting and the Lee Jofa damask on the armchair. **RIGHT:** Zajac and Callahan say, "We always start clients with a collection. It gives them a chance to search for wonderful things they know about." Here, the duo introduced vessels made of black-glazed terra-cotta from the late nineteenth and early twentieth centuries.

ABOVE: An upholstered screen gives the living room a cozy, private feeling. The sofa is covered in Rose Cumming's Fairoak chintz. The large-pillowed sofa, Régence chairs, and ottoman, upholstered in a Clarence House cotton-and-linen velvet, provide comfortable seating.
RIGHT: Inspired by the bold colors of English country house entry halls, the designers painted the foyer a brilliant orange. The curtain fabric, Cerise, is from Rose Cumming. Zajac designed the valance. The blue opaline Edwardian chandelier is from Objets Plus in Manhattan. **OPPOSITE:** Zajac created the dining room wallcovering, which looks like shelves displaying a collection of Chinese porcelains, by layering custom-designed papers and cutouts. Florence Zajac, the designer's mother, made the side chair frames, which are upholstered in Ivana, a Rose Cumming chintz. The multi-colored silk tufts are from Scalamandré.

ABOVE: An antique Portuguese bed with extravagantly turned wood posts and headboard, from J. Garvin Mecking in New York, prompted the feminine look of a daughter's bedrooms. Zuber & Cie's faux-lace wallpaper and Brunschwig & Fils's paper ribbon trim and cream taffeta soften the bold design and dark colors of a bedspread made from Mosaico, a Clarence House weave.
RIGHT: The master bedroom contains a bed with a canopy inspired by a valance in a Venetian palazzo. Lace from Henry Cassen is layered over yellow silk from Christopher Norman. The glass-bead fringe and wallpaper are from Brunschwig & Fils. The flower-patterned carpet is from Stark Carpet. **OPPOSITE:** Zajac and Callahan custom design every detail from finial to flooring, including the many elements used in the library paneling. They use as many patterns, trimmings, and techniques as possible to create their trademark charming and fanciful style.

ARTS AND CRAFTSMEN

Shingle style is one of American design's vernacular traditions, a legacy of practical luxury left by those large, turn-of-the-last-century beach "cottages" that dot the Atlantic coast. This never-out-of-style style has lasted into the new century, as Caroline Hirsch's house shows. Hirsch, the founder and owner of Caroline's Comedy Club in New York City, wanted a weekend place where she and lawyer Andrew Fox could relax year-round with friends and family.

Local architect Francis Fleetwood and New York interior designer Glenn Gissler designed her 9,000-square-foot, three-story, cedar-shingle-clad retreat to look as if it long belonged at the beach. The two craftsmen appropriated a variety of late-nineteenth-century elements—from porches, facade details, and, of course, shingles, to the wood paneling and neutral palette of many Arts and Crafts interiors—to create that illusion of history. As a result, all the modern conveniences, including multizone air conditioning, sophisticated stereo and television systems, lighting controls, and in-wall vacuuming, effectively disappear behind the period warmth of the generously proportioned rooms.

Gissler has concocted this new type of old-fashioned design by using details and ideas borrowed from the Shaker and Mission styles, as well as antiques suitable to the rooms of the English, Scottish, and Irish Arts and Crafts era. He says, "The look is the nineteenth century and early twentieth century cleansed of pattern. I wanted to draw on what I felt was the essence of the Arts and Crafts movement and emphasize the few things that defined the style."

Gissler describes the design process as one of reduction rather than addition, working to bring the house's large rooms down to what he calls a "comfortable" scale. "The look is not as simple or as rustic as the Mission or Arts and Crafts style," he adds. "It's urbane but not fancy, and although it's not humble, it's not showy, either. It's the nineteenth and early twentieth century cleansed of all of its pattern." Gissler designed the dining room lights and table. The chairs are from Newel Art Galleries in Manhattan.

ABOVE: In the library, Dutch Colonial Indonesian chairs from the 1920s pull up to an Austrian walnut table from 1910. Finding the right lamps for the house was a major challenge. The library's French iron wall sconces are from Reymer-Jourdan Antiques. The painting, *Big World,* is by Mark Innerst. **OPPOSITE:** In the living room, neutral fabrics complement the patterned, earth-tone rugs and dark furniture and floors. A custom-made, high-backed sofa is covered in a cotton velvet from Bergamo and detailed with cord and fringe.

ABOVE: Gissler opted for a strong, graphic statement. In the living room, the sofa, covered in wool from Coraggio, and the armchairs, in a rayon-and-nylon fabric from Payne Fabrics, are from Jonas Upholstery. The Louis XIII chair is from Reymer-Jourdan Antiques. The Dutch Colonial low table is from Renee Antiques. The rug is from Safavieh Carpets.

LEFT: A 1920s chandelier hangs in the foyer, where banquettes overlook the view. Francis Fleetwood, an East Hampton-based architect, designed the rambling, 9,000-square-foot, three-floor house, adapting the design from the turn-of-the-century American Shingle style, but giving it more windows and light.

ABOVE: Gissler was inspired by the simplicity and clean palette of a Shaker meetinghouse, and by a typically English Arts and Crafts room designed in 1903 by Frank Dickinson. In the master bedroom, he designed a dramatic mahogany bed with paneled head- and footboards based on drawings that provided historical precedents. Flanking the bed are a pair of Colonial West Indian tables. The draperies were made by Maury Shor, Inc., with cotton taffeta fabric from Decorators Walk. **RIGHT:** In the kitchen, an electrified oil lamp hangs above a trestle table. The English chairs are from Newel Art Galleries.

SWING TIME

In the decorative arts, a pendulum perpetually swings between more and less. Ornament, that is. As each style succeeds the one before, and as each style is absorbed into the tradition, the definition of more or less adjusts to contemporary perceptions. Art Deco, for example, now considered a paradigm of glamour and luxury, was in its own time considered a stripped-down reaction to the florid nature of Art Nouveau. Architect Salvatore LaRosa of New York's B Five Studio considers it a "style that contemporized Louis XV and Louis XVI French furniture, which is still considered the best furniture ever done." He should know. He spent the past several summers renovating a 2,300-square-foot residence in one of Manhattan's landmark Art Deco buildings.

Actually, the period influence came from his clients: she is the president of a dance foundation and editor of *2wice,* a dance and culture magazine; he is a prominent investment adviser. Having amassed collections of paintings (Robert Rauschenberg, Roy Lichtenstein, Willem de Kooning, and Richard Diebenkorn), vintage photographs, Christofle vases, Lalique glass, and Bakelite, the two were committed to integrating them into an Art Deco framework: "The coherence of living in an Art Deco–furnished apartment in an Art Deco building had a special appeal for us. Our children are members of the fourth generation to live in this building."

Dark woods, light velvets and silks, and bold art provide a foil for more demure details. Like some of the furniture—a Jacques-Émile Ruhlmann armchair and desk, chairs by Süe et Mare, a cabinet by Clement Mere—the apartment radiates poise and formality through precise craftsmanship and refined, precious materials.

ABOVE: LaRosa used large-scale artwork and mirrors for dramatic effect. *Ocean Park #23,* a 1969 painting by Richard Diebenkorn, hangs on the wall between the living and dining rooms. An untitled work by Donald Judd is in the background. B Five Studio designed the polished macassar ebony dining table. The vase is Gubbio pottery. Instead of a chandelier, a 1961 mobile by Alexander Calder hangs over the table. The vintage French Art Deco chairs are upholstered in a woven leather from Dualoy. **OPPOSITE:** Collections of period pieces, including these vases from Christofle and Linossier from Primavera in Manhattan, reinforce the Art Deco look.

ABOVE: B Five Studio assembled stylish furniture, rich textiles, and modern art to create an interior that recalls the
fine lines, luxury, and elegance characteristic of the Art
Deco period. LaRosa and Bob Vogel, his B Five Studio asso-
ciate, also custom designed some superior pieces of furniture, as well as rugs and cabinetry, to expand on the
clients' superb collection of originals and several other
standouts from the period that were selected for the project. "We were influenced by the tradition of the great
cabinetmakers," LaRosa says, referring to the pieces he
and his colleague designed. Included among the architects'
efforts is a chaise covered in a Jack Lenor Larsen velvet
and trimmed with a Jim Thompson silk. The pillow is made
of Clarence House's St. Laurent silk. The silk throw is from
Portantina, in Manhattan. ABOVE RIGHT AND OPPOSITE:
In the master bedroom, the wall of mirrored closet doors is
both functional and light enhancing. A delicate, sophisticated palette of neutrals and soft pinks is enlivened by the
graceful lines that the dark woods of the furniture etch in
space. A 1977 oil on paper by Willem de Kooning hangs
above the bed, which is draped in a nineteenth-century
Aubusson carpet. A 1992 Claes Oldenburg drawing hangs
near the Ruhlmann chair from the 1930s in the foreground
(and, opposite, reflected in the mirror), which is upholstered
in Mekong silk from Jim Thompson. RIGHT: In the small
dressing room off the bedroom, Christofle and Linossier
vases sit atop a rolltop cabinet designed by B Five Studio.

Pale wooden shelves and cabinetry unify the rooms. B Five Studio designed the study's Deco-style combination table and cabinet. LaRosa calls the ottoman, which tucks underneath and is upholstered in pig suede from Hermès, a "hostess stool" on which "the lady of the house can perch and carry on the obligatory conversation." The T. H. Robsjohn-Gibbings armchair is covered in matching suede. The clients' collections, including vintage black-and-white photographs, plastic pocketbooks, and Bakelite bangles, not only play off one another, they are integrated into the room's Art Deco framework.

ABOVE: In the living room, a Jacques-Émile Ruhlmann armchair is pulled up to one of his masterpieces, a 1923 macassar-ebony, ivory, and shagreen desk. **BELOW:** The living room sofa displays the sophisticated mix of textures that LaRosa has pulled together for this apartment. The rectangular pillow is covered in a Clarence House silk, the round pillow in a linen damask from Brunschwig & Fils. The Fendi throw is edged with chinchilla rosettes. "So much care was given to dressing tables, bars, even cocktail shakers—I aspire to that lifestyle," says the client, referring to the craftsmanship of Art Deco.

ABOVE: The living room floor is covered with a custom-made wool-and-silk oval Rope Scroll rug from V'soske. The dark-wood side chairs are by Süe et Mare. The Jacques-Émile Ruhlmann armchairs from Tony DeLorenzo, in New York, are upholstered in Clarence House's Izmir Silk. Hanging on the walls are a 1950 painting by William Baziotes and a 1937 drawing by Fernand Léger. Metal-mesh shades are made by Handwoven Studio to withstand the glare of the sun. **OPPOSITE:** LaRosa says, "Each piece has its own personality," like the Ruhlmann chair and the Oldenburg drawing in the bedroom, "and there is a conversation happening among them."

NEW INTERNATIONAL

Combining the new frontier spirit of the 1930s and 1940s with today's desire for sophisticated comfort and urbanity yields a timeless, ageless style.

PLANE GEOMETRY

MASTER PLAN

SPARE NECESSITY

DAY FOR NIGHT

Design is Darwinian. Nothing generates spontaneously. History always matters. And it repeats itself, subject to adaptation over time. Take, for example, New International Style.

When architectural historian Henry-Russell Hitchcock and Philip Johnson first spotted the origin of the species in 1930 and 1931, they were motoring around Europe at the behest of Alfred H. Barr, director of the Museum of Modern Art, searching for a new design typology. The International Style: Architecture Since 1922, their 1932 MoMA exhibition and accompanying catalog, introduced the work of Le Corbusier, Walter Gropius, Mies van der Rohe, and other modern architects to America. Hitchcock's catalog essay proposed a clear taxonomy of the style: an emphasis on volume, regularity, the intrinsic elegance of materials, technical perfection, and fine proportions; it outlawed applied ornament.

Today's New International Style exhibits these characteristics, with variations. It recombines the decorative arts tradition with the form-follows-function formula. It reabsorbs the visual harmonies, material luxuries, and physical comforts proposed by Jean-Michel Frank, Eileen Gray, Jacques-Émile Ruhlmann, and other designers of the '20s, '30s, and '40s who pursued simplicity along a path less reductive and with goals less grand than their Olympian architect contemporaries.

New International Style makes the modern movement modern again. It's about natural selection, and the survival of the fittest designs.

OPPOSITE: Tom Ford and Richard Buckley live in a Paris apartment filled with modern classics.

PLANE GEOMETRY

As with all things in New International Style, time-lessness, not timeliness, is the desired result. Form stripped to essence provides one means of transcending, but not denying, past and present. For Mexican architect Ricardo Legorreta, a master of geometry and the poetry of color, tangible Euclidean rigor creates a livable continuum of physical fact. Each of his commissions, including this Los Angeles house for an investment banker and his family, demonstrates an elegant proof for the lightness of being.

Los Angeles interior designer Kerry Joyce collaborated on this project with Legorreta. In Joyce's work, too, time factors into style. "I wanted the house to look as if it could have been done sixty years ago or today," he says. Since the owners' taste tends to the sleek and modern, Joyce has developed an interior idiom derived from French designs dating from the 1930s. A longtime Jean-Michel Frank–ophile, Joyce loves the comfort, simplicity, and luxury of Frank's designs, and finds them appropriate for Legoretta's light-filled, color-framed spaces. "Frank," he says, "is modern but friendly."

A Paris jaunt helped convince clients who were already disposed to Frank's reductive but hospitable aesthetic. But, Joyce explains, "the feeling we were after was not fleshed out until that magic day when they really understood the elegance of what are essentially simple shapes executed in fine materials." With vintage pieces hard to come by, Joyce has designed new furniture inspired by Frank and André Arbus, a Frank contemporary. Applying vellum to cabinet faces, using leather and silk velvet for upholstery, and employing ceruse, a high-contrast pigment, to transform wood grains, he has remade modern—again.

Kerry Joyce designed most of the furnishings himself, including those in the living room. Inspired by French masters from the 1930s and 1940s, particularly Jean-Michel Frank and André Arbus, he focused on the details, and used luxe, but quiet, materials, such as vellum, leather, and silk, in a palette that contrasts dark and light. The wood finish of choice is ceruse, a high-contrast pigment that accentuates the grain.

ABOVE: Joyce furnished the living room in an understated fashion. The Doucet sofas, in Italian velvet from Coraggio textiles, are from James Jennings Furniture. The Cee chairs and the Morgan floor lamps are both part of the Kerry Joyce Collection, also from James Jennings Furniture. The wool-and-silk rug is from Hokanson, Los Angeles. **LEFT:** The house for an investment banker and his family was designed by Mexican architect Ricardo Legorreta, who is celebrated for both his rigorous use of geometry, which creates dramatic spaces both inside and out, and for his luminous, hot-colored palette.

Joyce's furniture designs, including his sleek, Vellum X cabinet and the curvaceous Cee chair, have a coordinated look. Throughout the house, cabinets are faced in vellum, and sofas and chairs are upholstered in buttery leather or soft silk velvet. Wood finishes match as well.

ABOVE: Legoretta's palette is as bold inside as out, and includes seductive violets, oranges, and pinks that permeate the textured stucco of walls, alcoves, and hallways. The Sofi table and André Arbus–inspired chairs, by Kerry Joyce for James Jennings Furniture, reflect the geometry of the dining room architecture. **RIGHT:** The kitchen, an efficiently designed workspace in the best International Style tradition, puts function first. **OPPOSITE:** The breakfast room features Trent X table and side chairs from Joyce's namesake collection at James Jennings Furniture. The chairs are covered in Savanna Chestnut from Caldelle Leather, Santa Monica, CA.

MASTER PLAN

Twentieth-century design is about the plan. Spatial logic exists, and it demonstrates that conflicting propositions are not mutually exclusive. For example: If a downtown loft, then no views of Central Park. If views of Central Park, then no downtown loft. True? Not exactly. Of course, it's impossible to live in TriBeCa and on Central Park simultaneously. But some people can have the best of both worlds. The 3,000-square-foot apartment that Bruce Bierman, the Manhattan-based interior designer, has created for a fashion industry executive proves it.

First, the architecture: Bierman has transformed the ten-room apartment in an Art Deco building on the park by demolishing walls to encourage an easy spatial flow. Sliding panels can separate rooms that, when not divided, open to long vistas. "Because my client lives alone," Bierman explains, "there was no need for a lot of doors, but I still wanted to provide a sense of privacy when necessary."

In the process, Bierman has crafted a comfortable, technologically up-to-date interior for someone who can come home, put up his feet, and watch sports. "I wanted the style of the apartment to be appropriate to the site, but I had to find a way to incorporate all the technology my client wanted." Switch-laden panels installed by the front door, near the bed in the master suite, and in the coffee table provide access to controls monitoring lights, sound, and air-conditioning. Clean lines, neutral fabrics, and striking objects stand out in white-painted contexts. Amply proportioned sofas and chairs offer comfort, while delicate side tables and accessories add glamour.

The Art Deco–style custom chaise, with Amboina burl, faux ivory inlay, and nickel feet, refers to the building's past while remaining in the present. The upholstery fabric is Angora Mohair from J. Robert Scott. White walls provide an understated background in keeping with the spirit of rooms by two of the client's favorite designers, Art Deco masters Jacques-Émile Ruhlmann and Jean-Michel Frank.

ABOVE: Full-height folding panels of white laminated glass in mahogany frames separate the dining room from the bedroom, while a half-height folding screen divides the dining room from the living room. The anegré-veneered dining table is from Dakota Jackson. Chairs with dark-stained maple details are from Mattaliano. **LEFT:** In the living room, cushy custom seating upholstered with a J. Robert Scott fabric invites a kick-off-your-shoes attitude. The custom coffee table hides a television projector and control panel for lights, sound, and air-conditioning. **OPPOSITE:** A large nineteenth-century dog painting hangs over the custom sofa and three 1930s tables from Makassar-France.

ABOVE: The master bathroom uses an Art Deco palette of white marble, black granite, and silver accents, including the hardware and mirror frames, like the one from J. Pocker & Son over the tub. **LEFT:** Technology is ever-present, and integrated into the design. In the master bedroom, a control panel has been built into the custom headboard. The furniture is custom, and made of sapele. **OPPOSITE:** The master bedroom includes a sitting area. The custom club chair, in the manner of Jean-Michel Frank, is upholstered in Angora Mohair Birch from J. Robert Scott. The two-tiered telephone table from Karl Springer is covered in python skin. The metal frieze is a facade fragment from the old Best & Co. building on Fifth Avenue. The area rug is from Patterson, Flynn, Martin & Manges, New York.

SPARE NECESSITY

Plainness, says Thomas O'Brien, is passé. O'Brien ought to know. As the owner of New York–based Aero Studios, he is one of the leading proponent of New International Style, and the man who conceived the sophisticated and unexpected interiors of Toronto art gallery owner Sandra Simpson's bold, modern, steel-framed house.

Designed by Toronto architect Donald McKay, the 6,000-square-foot, three-story structure combines engineering bravado with fiercely plain detailing. Red I-beams span large rooms that relate to one another in a way that McKay calls "the tradition of unapologetic modern buildings." Commonplace materials cede the spotlight to Simpson's art collection. "Drywall is great if you're installing art, because it's strong and can easily be repainted," McKay points out.

O'Brien explains that Simpson runs her modern house in a formal way, in the grand tradition of the late nineteenth and early twentieth centuries. But this does not mean she adopts either a to-the-manor-born look, he says, or the unrelenting rigors of modernist sticklers. "I wanted the house to be simple and understandable, but I didn't want it to be so plain that it was totally flat," O'Brien insists. "In the end, it has to be human."

O'Brien's decorating decisions clearly accommodate both Simpson's art and her lifestyle. The Aero way generally tends to the more sensual moderns. "I am always inspired by Eileen Gray and Jean-Michel Frank," O'Brien says. Although celebrating the design luminaries of the 1930s and 1940s, O'Brien also pursues the uncommon mix. In Simpson's house, that respectful irreverence translates to such unexpected elements as late-nineteenth-century metal carts, vintage architects' tools, and a rusty farm trough, alongside soft, elegant textiles.

Red I-beams define different spaces within the open plan. In the living room, Allan McCollum's *Collection of 60 Drawings* provides a focal point. O'Brien had the ottoman, by architect Donald McKay, reupholstered. The lamp on the side table is from Aero.

ABOVE: Back-to-back sofas divide the living room. Inspired by an Eileen Gray piece, O'Brien designed the sofa and covered it in a Clarence House cotton. Antique fencing masks sit on the end table. The Stickley Mission chairs are from Peter-Roberts Antiques, Inc. **LEFT:** The house architect Donald McKay designed is unapologetically modern and built with commonplace materials. The kitchen, living room, and dining room are on the ground floor; the second floor contains the lower library and small living room; the upper library, master bedroom, and terrace are on the third floor. **OPPOSITE:** O'Brien's mix is uncommon and frankly but sensuously modern. The parchment X lamp by Jean-Michel Frank is from Maxfield, Los Angeles. O'Brien's own versions of designs from the 1930s and 1940s have classic proportions. His celadon velvet club chair, available through Aero, is a Frank-inspired design. Luxurious fabrics, in a neutral palette, provide textural interest throughout the house.

ABOVE: The dining room has a table and buffet designed by McKay. The vintage oak library chairs are from the owner's collection. The chrome Desny lamps are from George Kovacs. On the wall is Robert Fones's *Egyptian Expanded H/In the Compound,* a 1990 photograph on aluminum. RIGHT: Subtle fabrics make the master bedroom serene. Custom made by Aero, the armchair and ottoman are upholstered in Collobrieres from Pierre Frey. The custom wool carpet is from A. Morjikian Co.; the duvet fabric is from Manuel Canovas. BELOW: In the bathroom, the towels and rugs are from Portico, NY.

DAY FOR NIGHT

According to Gucci designer Tom Ford, who shares this pied-à-terre with writer Richard Buckley, finding a Paris apartment wasn't easy. The pair looked at more than 120 places before they found this one, which was built as a home in the eighteenth century and converted to apartments in the nineteenth. The place needed work, but it had 15-foot ceilings and a view of the Seine.

While Ford has created an aggressive image for Gucci, his aesthetic at home is more restrained. "We're both sort of modernist freaks," he explains. "We like Philip Johnson's Glass House, Mies van der Rohe, and the California architects, especially Neutra. But what we now call modern, of course, looked totally normal until the 1980s and modern went out of fashion."

"I have a really hard time living with color," Ford says. "It demands too much from me, and from the room. I can't even sleep at night knowing there's a colorful pair of shoes in the closet." So they replastered and repainted in a muted palette, but left the walls' ruffled woodwork, which Buckley calls "pastry," untouched. Parquet floors were stained a dark oak. And they built a stainless-steel kitchen.

They furnished their rooms with twentieth-century pieces, plus the occasional accessory from the Gucci Home Collection. "In essence, this is an old French apartment stripped of color, and edited with compositions of objects we love," explains Ford. "We could have stripped everything, but we wanted to feel that we were in Paris when we were in Paris. It's modern, but in context."

Ford and partner, Richard Buckley, are die-hard modernists with a taste for the sybaritic, as their Paris pied-à-terre proves. The furnishings mix twentieth-century classics by the likes of Mies van der Rohe and Charles Eames with witty, glamorous pieces in chrome and Lucite.

RIGHT: The neutral background of the dining room sets off strong shapes, such as the over-scale light fixture, the Ford-designed dining table of travertine and limed oak, and Jacques Quine's glass-and-bronze console tables. **OPPOSITE:** Andy Warhol's "Shadow" paintings inspired the color of the library, which contains a Chinese goatskin rug from Gucci Home, a Knoll sofa, a Mies-designed table, and a fiberglas Eames chair from 1948.

BELOW: Ford and Buckley replastered and repainted, leaving the wood ornament, or "pastry," as Buckley calls it, on the walls. The parquet floors were stained a dark oak. Ford designed the chaise in the living room. A German Arts and Crafts table from the 1920s is combined with Mies van der Rohe chairs. OPPOSITE: The library shows off the negative version of the black-and-white palette, with dark floors and walls, and white furnishings and accents. Classic designs, as well as art, objects, and photographs were collected from dealers and flea markets.

COUNTRY LUXE

Here's a way to celebrate family and fun, surf and sun, and any place that can come alive with the joy of decoration.

COTTAGE INDUSTRY

URBANITY À LA PROVENÇAL

CHINA BY THE SEA

EAST COAST MEETS WEST COAST

Mixing metaphors is fun. So when it comes to country luxe, expect the unexpected. The decorating world's answer to designer jeans, country luxe parties hard, travels widely, and wears well. And it has a history. When the Romans escaped the city for the summer, they flocked to their houses and estates in Pompeii. Centuries later, Palladio dotted the Veneto with lavishly decorated neoclassical villas, many of which were also working farms. One of these Greco-Roman structures, the Villa Rotonda, provided a model for Monticello, and for many plantations of the American South. The great English estates have for centuries offered a paradigm of elegant country living, approximated by the French and by prerevolutionary Russians.

But so much for the aristocracy and the landed gentry. After the Industrial Revolution, newly leisured classes established a revolutionary pattern and went on vacation, building elegant second—or third or fourth—homes for occasional use. Hence Newport's cottages, the great camps of the Adirondacks, and McKim, Mead & White's rambling Shingle-style houses up and down the East Coast.

Country Luxe today is just as exuberant but, in the spirit of casual Fridays, a lot less formal. Life is good. So why not celebrate, and decorate?

OPPOSITE: Diamond-Baratta designed this beach house with custom details that create a family portrait.

COTTAGE INDUSTRY

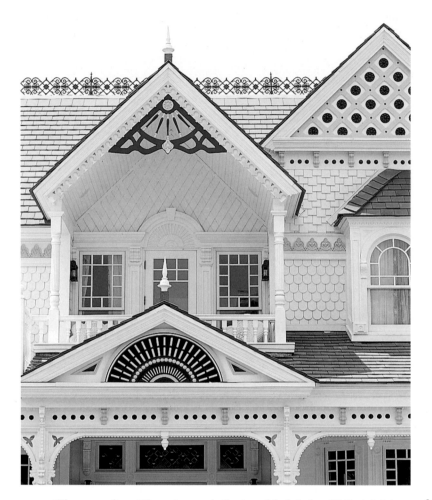

There are cottages, and then there are cottages. The sprawling, Victorian-style "painted lady" that Philadelphia designers Judie and Bennett Weinstock constructed from the ground up falls into the second category. In a New Jersey resort town, on a quarter-acre plot just yards from the ocean, between basketball hoops and barbecue grills, the Weinstocks have built their dream house. In the wicker-dotted wraparound porches, the crisp white fretwork, and a shiny, red-tiled roof, these two Anglophiles have enshrined the lighter side of a ponderous period. What, after all, is more Victorian than eccentricity?

They call the house the Quilted Cottage, Bennett explains, "because we have long had a love affair with quilts. So it seemed appropriate to focus our attention on the color, pattern, and fantasy of quilting." The two dreamed up each one of the countless details, from the cutouts on steps, stoops, and porches to the pineapple finials to the fabric-covered tissue boxes and wastebaskets that coordinate with the color schemes of every room. Their collection of rare doll-sized quilts inspired the interior's obsessive leitmotif, which is also found in complex stencil designs on oak floors, in color ideas for custom-woven rugs, and in leaded- and stained-glass windowpanes.

The Weinstocks profess to have gotten "the whimsy out of our systems," and insist that they are now "going to relax and enjoy the house." As Judie says, "We take the time to do the gracious things." That's now the industry in this cottage.

ABOVE: The Weinstocks built their Victorian cottage in about nine months. Designer Victor Pisani drew every bit of Victorian ornamentation in advance. Most elements were made of Fypon, a woodlike polymer product that withstands the shore's salty air.
OPPOSITE: The Weinstocks delight in pattern, and the more the better, especially in the master bedroom, which layers floral on floral and plaid on plaid. The salon set in the alcove includes a settee with a cutout back.

ABOVE: In the family room, paintings by Howard Finster (left) and Mose Tolliver, and chairs covered in Potomac Linen Check fabric by Brunschwig & Fils flank an American painted kas. **RIGHT:** Joanne Hudson Associates of Philadelphia designed the kitchen, complete with yellow, blue, and white wall and counter tiles set in a quilt design. The La Cornue stove is from France. Patinated yellow custom cabinetry from Wm. Ohs, which matches the glass-fronted cabinets, conceals the Sub-Zero refrigerator and freezer.

ABOVE: Most of the rooms in the Quilted Cottage were designed around quilt patterns. The master bedroom is furnished with faux bamboo pieces. The upholstered chair is covered in Kenmore by Scalamandré. The carpet is from Stark. RIGHT: The Weinstocks relished the challenge of merging Victorian ornamentation with modern necessities, such as switchplates and air-conditioning ducts. They hired decorative painter Meg Shay to disguise them to blend in with the tile and wallpaper. Tiles depicting cats are a frieze in the grandchild's bathroom. OPPOSITE: The powder room was designed around a nineteenth-century French sink stand. The antique mirror frame is English. Bathroom fixtures have been nickel-plated to prevent deterioration in the salt air.

URBANITY À LA PROVENÇAL

Everyone knows the elements of Provençal style: sun-dried colors, sun-dried herbs, rustic pavers, and a peculiarly golden light. But the spirit of Provence is more than just a formula. The interior that Paris-based Jacques Grange has designed for Terry and Jean de Gunzburg proves it. Grange, who has had a house in Provence for years, tipped off the de Gunzbergs that a *mas* (a typical Provençal farmhouse) was available a few miles from his own. After they acquired it, he set about renovating it. "I like to make houses come alive," he says.

The de Gunzburgs and Grange cite three elements for the project's success. "We did everything with emotion, sensitivity, and time," says Terry, who, like Grange, was intent on keeping the rural aspect of the property intact. "I wanted to transform the *mas* without taking away its rural soul," explains Grange. That meant reinventing the use of the region's time-honored materials but avoiding the usual seductive clichés, such as peach-colored stucco walls and terra-cotta-tiled floors.

Grange mastered rusticity by contrasting very rough materials with extremely sophisticated objects. He also reintroduced *cocho pesto*, a traditional Italian technique that encrusts marble mosaic in terra-cotta. While celebrating local materials and colors, Grange has expanded the aesthetic of the South of France by embracing a modern Mediterranean mix. Designs by Jean-Michel Frank, Georges Braques, the Giacometti brothers, and Eugene Prinz take on a new allure in these surroundings. "It's not enough to find beautiful things," says Grange. "One must be able to see how they can fit into a home and provide the necessary sense of intimacy."

In the wood-beamed living room, a 1962 portrait of Marilyn Monroe by Bert Stern focuses the eye on the overscale mantelpiece. The 1950 ebony tray by Alexandre Noll, the 1940 Cazaux bowl on the Italian marquetry table, and the 1940s American andirons are all from Galerie du Passage in Paris. The antique rocking chair is from Canada.

ABOVE: Grange used local materials in unusual ways. The Jean-Michel Basquiat painting makes a bold statement, as does a coal scuttle shaped like a giant cricket. **LEFT:** The living room exemplifies Grange's mix of pieces from the 1930s and the 1950s and rough-hewn materials. The linen-covered sofa is custom designed. The armchair is by T. H. Robsjohn-Gibbings. Objects by Georges Jouve sit on a 1930s table in front of a 1930s French screen from Malmaison Antiques in Manhattan. Portuguese tiles frame the window and a Japanese mat covers the floor.

ABOVE: The client loves color, and filled the kitchen with Provençal-hued table-cloths, napkins, dishes, and glasses. On the backsplash and kitchen walls, Grange arranged French glass tiles and Portuguese painted tiles in an unusual combination. The colors are echoed on the cabinet knobs. **OPPOSITE:** Grange extended the riot of color into the dining room. The vintage Thonet chairs and the 1930s table are from Galerie du Passage in Paris. The nineteenth-century Turkish lantern is from Malmaison Antiques in Manhattan. The ornate metal-and-glass lantern serves as a foil for the clean lines of the Thonet chairs and complements the colorful tiles in the kitchen. The Swedish rug is from the Galerie Eric Philippe in Paris. Wooden lattice doors between the dining and living rooms create privacy but allow for air circulation.

ABOVE: For the master bedroom, the de Gunzbergs wanted a big, open, loftlike space. They commissioned artist Vincent Corbière, who shows his work at the Galerie Pierre Passebon in Paris, to design the headboard and night tables specifically for this room. **LEFT:** In the study, a ceramic bull by Morel stands on a 1937 column capital made of wood. The bookcase, from the 1930s, is by Jean-Michel Frank. **OPPOSITE:** Jacques Grange designed the two-tone mosaic wall tiles in the sitting room. The geometric pattern uses a traditional Italian technique called *cocho pesto,* in which marble mosaic is encrusted in terra-cotta. The vintage leather armchair, designed by Alberto Giacometti for Jean-Michel Frank, is from the Galerie Arc en Seine in Paris. The chest is a 1950s design by Jean Royère purchased from the Galerie du Passage. The rug, from the Galerie Vallois, is based on a design by Georges Braque. Woven horsehair fabric was applied to the doors to create a neutral surface.

CHINA BY THE SEA

A beach house means different things to different people. Some opt for sand and stripes, others for white canvas and pine. This 15,000-square-foot East Hampton house, designed by John Barman and Jack Levy of New York's John Barman, Inc., is about exuberance, thanks to a client with a mind of her own. "She likes bright colors, as I do," Barman says, going on to explain that the client "specifically requested a palette of blues and yellows. In the bedroom, she wanted gray. And she asked for a Chinese orientation overall, because, as she said, 'It's a serious house. I want to make it fun, but with quality furniture.'"

As a result, the house is awash in color and light, from the double-height entry hall to the dining room, library, master bedroom, guest bedrooms, and children's rooms. The blue-and-yellow theme threads though the interiors, in floor coverings, drapery and upholstery fabrics, and accessories picked up on two trips to England. When Barman and Levy found the vermilion lacquer chairs now sitting in the front hall, their decisive client pronounced, à la Diana Vreeland, "Red is my neutral. It comes from hanging around you."

Chinese patterns and influences abound. Rooms are detailed with bamboo-patterned curtain rods in a variety of finishes; Chinese-style prints upholster walls, sofas, and chairs; and a giant dragon sweeps across the floor in a custom rug.

The library, in a departure from the dominant theme, takes its motif directly from the sea. The lighthouse-shaped octagonal room is paneled in waxed mahogany, and sports a rope-covered chandelier. This is the country, after all, and a little flexibility is in order.

The Chinese painting established the living room's palette. The fabrics are from Etro. The rug is a custom Portuguese needlepoint. The bamboo detail of the antique fireplace screen matches that of the custom curtain rods from P.E. Guerin.

ABOVE: Barman and Levy used the client's love of strong color and chinoiserie to make this beach house truly exuberant. Four custom-made Chinese figurines on custom-made stands guard the entrance to the dining room and the entry hall (left and opposite). The red-lacquered dining room chairs are Chinese Chippendale; the table is early nineteenth-century English. The chandelier is from Richter. **LEFT:** A custom rug from Stark dominates the double-height entry hall. The lantern is from Charles Edwards, London. Barman, whose love for red is celebrated, notes his client insisted on the red hall chairs by saying, "Red's my neutral. I got it from hanging around you." The two early-nineteenth-century English wing chairs are classically upholstered in button-tufted red leather. Two antique Chinese silk banners of ancestral figures hang on high. **OPPOSITE:** Stark custom-made the stair runner.

RIGHT: The master bathroom has his-and-hers pedestal sinks and tiles from Waterworks. The bamboolike curtain rods are from P.E. Guerin. The curtain fabric is from Christopher Hyland. The ornamental mirror is Venetian. An early-nineteenth-century English recamier offers a place for lounging. **BELOW RIGHT:** One powder room features faux-painted bamboo trellis on the walls above white beadboard. The gilt wood mirror is Chinese Chippendale. The bamboo theme includes the sink, by Sherle Wagner. **BELOW LEFT:** In the second powder room, a yellow-painted Chinese chest from ABC Carpet & Home has been topped with marble and adapted to hold the sink.

The color palette and Chinese motifs are also found in the guest house. The red-lacquered faux-bamboo bedside table is custom. The bed cover and upholstery fabrics are from Clarence House. The custom rug from Stark matches the striped window fabric from Robert Allen. The faux-bamboo curtain rods from P.E. Guerin, used throughout the house, add another layer of detail.

EAST COAST MEETS WEST COAST

Forget about the differences between the vernacular architectural styles of America's two coasts. William Diamond and Anthony Baratta's large-scale renovation of and addition to this Long Island beach house takes the best of two worlds and makes something new. "We love California decorating," says Bill Diamond. "It's big, bold, and graphic. In this house, we've simplified it and taken it back to New England."

They converted the original structure, a 5,000-square-foot 1890s Shingle-style house, to an 11,000-square-foot complex for their longtime clients, a family of eight with two black Labradors. These are people who enjoy East Coast style on a West Coast scale. "They play every sport there is to play," Diamond says. "She's a phenomenal cook, and they are avid entertainers. They travel with friends, so the eleven bedrooms in this house are always full."

For the interior, the designers have abstracted the details of the Victorian original and blown them up to a new scale. "Victorian homes have porches with beautiful turned columns and carved brackets—we brought these exterior concepts inside, and made them big and bold," Diamond says. These pieces are carved and turned by hand, as are interior and exterior doors, with a combination of square and diamond mullions appropriate to the Victorian tradition.

"These are special clients," Diamond explains. "We've done ten homes for them in the last fifteen years. Working with them now is like shorthand."

LEFT: Diamond and Baratta designed the living room sofa's fabric with a pattern of buoys, lighthouses, and sailboats.
RIGHT: The 24-foot-high living room has a cupola, and windows on three sides. The custom rug, in the shape of a giant compass, has true points and a true center. The custom white wing chairs resemble old-fashioned Adirondack porch chairs. The unusually large golf painting over the fireplace, bought at auction in London, dates to 1906.

ABOVE LEFT: Modeled after a McKim, Mead & White original in a Newport, RI, house, the enormous Palladian window in the master bedroom overlooks a pond. The sofa (left) and wing chair in the master bedroom's seating alcove are covered in an custom fabric that Diamond calls a Maine scenic: "It's like a bird's-eye view of the water, lighthouses, houses, and trees, and the clients's beloved black labradors." The rug is hand-hooked and hand-braided, in an original technique developed by Baratta. The rug provides a virtual portrait of the family, depicting its favorite activities, one per circle: playing golf, going to the beach, playing tennis, the labs, going to church, at the windmill. **ABOVE:** The exterior rear elevation of the living room addition includes a massive brick structure for fireplace and chimney.

The kitchen and dining rooms, once exterior porches, are separated by a hand-carved archway that brings the porches' architectural features inside. Custom, old-wood paneling lines the kitchen, where an unmatched set of Hitchcock chairs from the 1820s–1860s surrounds the table. The dining room's Windsor chairs have pillows and lambrequins of handwoven, turquoise-plaid cotton.

ABOVE: The porch overlooks the pond. The custom, dog-proof screen doors include details from the Victorian era, like turned balustrades and gingerbread. The bistro chair and table are French. Custom lanterns, made in England, are painted bright blue. RIGHT: Custom tiles in the kitchen were designed to celebrate the family labradors and their little red tongues. OPPOSITE: The master bathroom opens off the bedroom, which is detailed with outdoor elements brought indoors, like the white-painted planking, chair rail, and balustrade, as well as a large, turned column that anchors one side of a bookcase. Two beachscapes hang outside the master bathroom, which features an antique English white ball-and-claw-footed tub and wide-plank walls finished in a grayish blue-green, like the side of a barn. A collection of antique weathervanes hangs behind the tub. The floor is marble.

MINIMALISM

When space and light are the greatest luxuries of all, a sublime simplicity is the best way to let the elements speak for themselves.

MACHINE FOR LIVING

LESS IS MORE

FORM FOLLOWS FUNCTION

TRUTH IN ARCHITECTURE

Truth is beauty, and beauty is truth. In Minimal Style, both are naked. And there's no faking it. So give Mies van der Rohe, the man who proclaimed that less is more, his due. Mies, Gropius, Le Corbusier, Aalto, and others in the pantheon of architects on the Olympus of modernism championed a rigorously analytical approach to the complex problems of space and structure, one in which form follows function, the house is a machine for living, and there is such a thing as truth in architecture.

The modern masters meant to change the world, not to make a style statement. But art will out. Their work demonstrates how a seemingly prosaic formula—a few vertical planes to divide space, built-in storage, and a contemporary chair or two—can actually define the sublime in three dimensions.

Minimal Style is a demanding mistress. It pursues the luxury of simplicity. It celebrates the revelation of essence.

OPPOSITE: Architect Michael Gabellini created harmony among colors and finishes in this elegant, spare penthouse.

MACHINE FOR LIVING

For New York architect Michael Gabellini, less is always more. Gabellini does not consider this sparely furnished Park Avenue penthouse in New York, for instance, to be minimal in the least. "It's opulent," he says. "The idea was to produce a pure space."

Gabellini believes that each interior should reflect its occupants the way a set animates its actors. These clients, he explains, wanted an environment for displaying their photography collection, which includes prints by Man Ray, Atget, Maholy-Nagy, Lissitzky, and Edward Weston. He gave them not only a space suitable for a gallery, but a tranquil, meditative, clutter-free residence. The husband calls the result "an apartment about light."

For Gabellini, light is "poetic and emotional. I treated the apartment like a camera aperture. You allow light in or close it down. You shape it and filter it." After demolishing walls to chart the daily path of light through the interior, Gabellini combined the two one-bedroom apartments into an environment with separate zones for public and private activities. "I thought of the public rooms—living room, dining room, library, and gallery—as exterior space. They are the stage. The kitchen and service rooms are backstage."

Gabellini's spatial composition consists of solids and voids sketched in black and white: plaster walls painted titanium white and accented by ebonized mahogany room dividers, honed limestone floors, and stainless-steel doors. The furniture, like the prints on the walls, was selected from the '30s and the '60s. Iconic modern designs by Eileen Gray, Poul Kjaerholm, and George Nakashima sit side by side with Gabellini's own spare forms for beds, tables, desks, and cabinets.

In Minimal Style, the details matter, and Gabellini has pared them to their essences. Corners and reveals are perfect; joints are flush; even radiator grills contribute to the purity of the space. The plaster walls are painted titanium white to capture the natural daylight. UV-filtered windows cut down on glare and protect the clients' collection of photographs. Each piece of furniture, whether from the 1930s or the 1960s, occupies the space like sculpture. Chosen like works of art, the furnishings include these classic modern chairs.

ABOVE: Spare and elegant, the furnishings include a Saporiti sofa and two Yoshio Taniguchi-designed chairs, reproductions commissioned after the clients admired the originals in Tokyo's Hotel Okura. The table is by Gabellini. The Marcel Duchamp portrait above the sofa is by Man Ray. **LEFT:** In the living room, an antique Thai torso sits on a limestone ledge. A Kjaerholm bench and a Gabellini-designed stainless-steel table made by Object Metal in Brooklyn, NY, complete the sitting area. The walls are designed to display photographs from a collection that spans the 1850s to the 1940s and includes prints by Stieglitz, Weston, Lissitzky, Rodchenko, Maholy-Nagy, Man Ray, and Mapplethorpe.

BELOW: Gabellini demolished the interior walls of the apartment to create an open stage of the living room, dining room, library, and gallery. He also chose materials with an eye for the subtle harmony of color and finish: satin-finish stainless steel (a Gabellini trademark), honed-finish bluestone for the dining table top, ebonized ribbon mahogany for dividing walls and some storage elements, honed-finish beige limestone for the floors. The walnut dining chairs are by George Nakashima. A mahogany-finished storage element fits neatly between interior columns that frame the dining room and kitchen. The top provides a serving surface, the drawers space for cutlery and linens.

OPPOSITE: The kitchen may be backstage, so to speak, but that does not mean it's been designed with different standards or with less elegant materials.

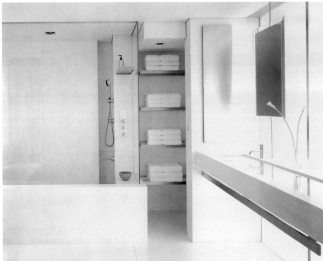

TOP: The bedroom is divided into zones for sleeping, bathing, and storage. Gabellini designed the bed of anegré wood with pull-out consoles that have push-button controls for sound, light, and shades. He and Greek colleague Stavros Neonakis designed the walnut bench with leather-thong webbing. A Mapplethorpe nude hangs on a ribbon mahogany wall that divides the bedroom from the dressing room. **ABOVE:** The glassed-in bath is made of hand-carved Yugoslavian marble. **RIGHT:** Wall-mounted Kroin faucets and a sweeping sink in the powder room contribute to the minimal aesthetic.

The master bathroom has electronic glass walls that change from transparent to opaque at the flip of a switch. Gabellini designed the sink, hand-carved in Yugoslavian white marble. The Kroin faucets have a custom satin nickel-plate finish.

LESS IS MORE

There's a kind of Yankee thrift expressed in the houses and farms of older New England. The spaces and the materials reveal an absolute integrity of intent joined to a wonderful economy in design. This indigenous version of "less is more" appealed to Barbara Dente and Donna Cristina, partners in a New York fashion consulting and advertising firm, when they began their transformation of this 1820 farmhouse in southeastern Connecticut.

Dente and Cristina take pleasure in spare, but not empty, rooms. They prefer clean lines, a nearly monochromatic palette, and a deliberate placement of the rig-

orously edited array of objects they've collected over the years on their many travels. Says Dente, "It's about taking away and refining, refining, refining."

Rather than initiating major construction, which might have disturbed the intimate scale of the house's small rooms, the two decided to simply square the spaces off, and in some cases to raise the ceilings. The wide-plank floors were sanded and stained dark brown; the consistent color of the floor leads the eye from one room to the next, and creates an illusion of expanded space.

Whether American, French, Italian, Irish, Welsh, Japanese, or Chinese, the objects that Dente and Cristina have amassed date, like the house itself, from the early nineteenth century. Hand-blown candlesticks, Tahitian shells, early photographs, silver letter openers, Indian stones, and handmade brooms, "come from different cultures," Dente says, "but often from what I call the more primitive side of the period. I like the cobbler's benches and baskets, not the things that belonged to kings and queens."

OPPOSITE: Dente and Cristina renovated their early-nineteenth-century Connecticut farmhouse, which sits at the center of a 27-acre property. **BELOW:** The renovation was all about proportion. Dente and Cristina squared off the rooms, and in some cases raised the ceilings. Taking pleasure in clean lines and a nearly monochromatic palette, and also paying minute attention to the placement of objects, they furnished the dining room sparely, with a Quaker meetinghouse table, wood chairs designed by Christian Liaigre, and a conical metal hanging lamp. Throughout they sanded the original wide-plank floors and then stained them dark brown.

BELOW LEFT: Lightfilled, white-painted rooms, almost monastic in their simplicity, contain objects, like this cobbler's bench, with strong, simple forms. **BOTTOM LEFT:** In the library, a Scottish Orkney Island chair cozies up to the fireplace. The late-nineteenth-century broom hails from the American South. **RIGHT:** A special kind of order, that of the educated and cultivated eye, creates a quality of serenity throughout the house. The two have so rigorously refined and edited their collections, and so carefully determined the specific place for each one of their treasures, that the interior seems deceptively simple, even easy. In the main living room, white walls set off the Christian Liaigre armchairs, lamps, and sofa from France. The things that Dente and Cristina favor date from the beginning of the nineteenth century. Their handblown candlesticks, early photographs, silver letter openers, Indian stones, and handmade brooms come from different cultures.

ABOVE LEFT: A cotton Marseilles spread envelopes a custom-made four-poster bed of fruitwood with an ebony finish. The metal bedside lamps are from the 1920s. **ABOVE:** The high-ceilinged sitting room contains twin daybeds made to order in Manhattan. **OPPOSITE:** Dente and Cristina made a new, spacious bathroom from two of the small rooms upstairs. Plumbing and installation was a challenge. To make the sink, they dropped a basin into a slab of Connecticut bluestone, which became a new top for an old pine table that stands in the center of the room. The old-fashioned looking shower-head and faucets are from Waterworks. The acrylic Japanese soaking tub was light enough to be installed on the second floor. **LEFT:** A second tabletop sink, which also has a basin in bluestone slab, stands against the bathroom's opposite wall.

FORM FOLLOWS FUNCTION

What's the cure for sensory overload? Many designers begin, and sometimes end, with white. They wipe the walls, the floors, the ceilings clean of distraction by finishing them with the absence of color. Judith Niedermaier, entrepreneurial president of Niedermaier Inc., the Chicago-based furnishings and display company, took this approach when she moved into one of Chicago's most elegant prewar buildings.

The 6,000-square-foot apartment that Niedermaier purchased in a 1928 landmark designed by Benjamin Marshall, the architect of the Drake Hotel, still sported the evidence of its last renovation, a lime green and bright harvest-gold palette that was chic in 1974. Working with local architect Mark Demsky, Niedermaier decided to leave most of the walls and doors intact in the large front rooms; a 30-by-30-foot living room features windows with panoramic views across Lake Michigan. The two did, however, reconfigure the back of the house, creating a master bedroom suite from three existing rooms. They also overhauled the kitchen.

The new interior celebrates white: in furniture frames and upholstery fabrics, in the sheepskin rugs and bleached wood floors, in the sleek plaster mantel and the whitewashed oak dining tables. Why? "Like many people in the design business," Niedermaier says, "I felt I needed a blank slate to come home to." Although she experiences the white drift of her public expanses as a tonic, she prefers neutrals—restful beiges and browns—for the bedroom. "White wakes me up too much," she explains. "I like something a little quieter for the bedroom, so I can sleep better."

OPPOSITE: Furnishings covered in white fabrics and whitewashed floors emphasize the airiness of Niedermaier's 30-by-30-foot living room. Aside from a white-painted Jean Royère floor lamp, all the furniture is by Niedermaier Inc. A fabric from Henry Calvin covers the sofa. Two armchairs, upholstered in a Manuel Canovas velvet, flank a coffee table designed by Jean-Pierre Tortil. The rug is sheepskin. BELOW: A fox rug adds texture and depth to the white space of the library. Venini glass vases sit atop the mantelpiece by architect Mark Demsky. The curved sofa, chair, and glass tables are from Neidermaier Inc.

ABOVE: Tall doors open onto the serene dining room, where three 52-inch-square whitewashed oak tables, designed for Neidermaier by Sean Scott, line up end to end. The leather-covered Deux chairs are from Niedermaier Inc. The painting is Christopher LeBrun's *Rider With Shadow.* **RIGHT:** Designed by Demsky and Niedermaier in collaboration with deGiulio Kitchen Design, a Chicago firm, the kitchen's modern detailing, natural materials, and pale palette is in keeping with the rest of the apartment. Open shelves conveniently store everyday china and glassware. The cabinetry, in a light maple laminate that has been topped with Corian, is from Siematic, as are the stainless steel bar pulls. The polished-chrome sink hardware is from BarWils.

Niedermaier, who finds vast expanses of white space bracing rather than calming, decided to use her favorite beiges and darker natural hues in the master bedroom suite, which
nevertheless has the same spare-but-luxurious aesthetic as the rest of the apartment. As
she says, "White wakes me up too much. I like something a little quieter for the bedroom." The limed oak walls create a serene cocoon. Jagtar silk fabrics from Kirk
Brummel were used for the tailored bedcover.

Neidermaier and Demsky created the large master bedroom and bathroom suite out of three existing rooms. A low wall of limed oak serves as a partition between the sink and the bathtub in the master bathroom. An Arne Jacobsen-designed Vola faucet, made by Kroin, is mounted above a polished-glass counter and sink from Vitraform. The exposed polished chrome plumbing is from Cherry Creek. The space also includes dressing and make-up areas that are simply but elegantly done.

TRUTH IN ARCHITECTURE

There is such a thing as an architectural point of view. Minimal Style requires it. Designer Jennifer Post has it in abundance. She describes it as follows: "You start from the elevation, instead of from the materials or furniture plan." That's the approach she used to turn a 3,200-square-foot, two-bedroom condominium on New York's Upper West Side into a free-flowing, light- and art-filled space.

Although the building was new, it required a complete renovation to achieve its current state of timelessness. Post says function came first: "People live in rooms for more than one reason, and use them for more than one function, especially in urban dwellings. Everything is articulated for a reason." The existing interior walls impeded the flow of light, one of the city's most prized luxuries, from the floor-to-ceiling windows on three of the four perimeter walls. A little demolition, and the installation of sand-blasted sliding glass doors as dividers, readjusted the balance and maximized the views of Central Park and the Hudson River.

New limestone floors and a palette of white finishes in various degrees of matte and gloss create a luminous envelope for an art collection that resonates with color. Post has opted for modern furnishings in the tradition of twentieth-century classics: leggy pieces with elegant lines. Clear, strong colors used judiciously in living, dining, and bedrooms further enliven the interior.

"People have always thought of minimal as cold, and classical as period or antique," Post says. "But things have changed, and now people look to professionals for timeless, classical design. They say, 'Wrap me in comfort, and keep it elegant, clean, and simple.'" And she does.

The dining room, says Post, is classical minimalism with some color. The whites in this space have a variety of finishes, from matte to high-gloss lacquer. The dining chairs, designed for outdoor use and made by Brown Jordan, are an unusual, rather off-beat choice, but their lyrical lines suit the room. The white glass-topped table is from Poliform, New York. The white Bosa bowl is from Property, New York. The Robert Motherwell hanging on the wall adds a dash of intense color. The floors are honed limestone.

ABOVE: Post opened the interior to take advantage of the views. The ceramic Bubble pot by Abigail Simpson is from Troy. The black Charlotte Pérriand chair is a re-edition from Donzella, New York. **LEFT:** Post wanted things to float in space, hence the cantilevered white lacquer shelves. **RIGHT:** The materials palette for the apartment is established in the foyer. *Reflection,* a bronze sculpture by Dimitry German through Grant Gallery, Manhattan, rests on a custom white lacquer stand.

ABOVE: The feeling of lightness carries through the apartment, in part because of the color palette and also because all of the furniture seems to float off the ground. In the master bedroom, Post knocked out all the previous closets to expand the available space. The white lacquer dressers are custom from Format, New York. The bed is by Molteni through Format. The bedding is from Frette. The carpet is Einstein Moomjy. The chair is by James Mont through Liz O'Brien.
LEFT: The master bathroom is tiled with limestone.
OPPOSITE: The black-and-white photograph is by Jack Sturges.

BOHEMIAN CHIC

There's nothing like art for art's sake, especially when the artist makes home a canvas to celebrate individuality, family, and life through design.

THE *PAINTER* AND THE *NOVELIST*

THE *MUSICIAN*

THE *FILMMAKER*

THE *DESIGNER*

Banish all images of freezing garrets and squalid rooms. The true bohemian still confidently flouts convention, but a possession-free existence in a haphazard habitat no longer signifies the only life worth living. For today's new bohemians, the home contains a collage of inspiration, experiment, memory, and personal expression.

European bohemians have long been celebrated for their distinctive homes. Misia Sert entertained her avant-garde friends in pattern-on-pattern-filled rooms memorialized on canvas by Edouard Vuillard. William Morris and his pre-Raphaelite colleagues at Kelmscott blurred the boundaries between art and craft. Bloomsburyites Vanessa Bell, Duncan Grant, and Dora Carrington extended a passion for ornament to objects, interiors, and gardens the way they did everything else, reflexively, like breathing. Edward James, Salvador Dali's patron, imparted luxe eccentricity to his three residences: West Dean; Monkton, whose surrealist interiors included a Dali-designed sofa in the shape and color of Mae West's lips; and Xilitla, his concrete city of dreams in Mexico.

Americans, by contrast, have tended toward the conventional at home. But there are a number of new bohemians who are redefining do-it-yourself decorating and exulting in the irreverent and the unusual. Their aesthetic sensibilities, while unique and idiosyncratic, are every bit as refined and deliberate as those of the most exalted decorators. Freed from brand names and manufactured elegance, they fill their rooms and their lives with things that, whatever their provenance, have personal meaning.

OPPOSITE: Judith Hudson's painter's eye delights in placing a vintage blue porcelain bathtub against yellow walls.

THE PAINTER AND THE NOVELIST

When painter Judith Hudson and novelist Richard Price moved with Annie and Genevieve, their two young daughters, into a Manhattan brownstone, Hudson's community of friends and fellow artists—including Julian Schnabel, Ricky Clifton, architect Pietro Cicognani, designer Kevin Walz—offered advice and inspiration about how to make the place their own. "Julian was there for a total of ten minutes and gave me sixty ideas," recalls Hudson, who assembled and subdued the riot of pattern and period throughout the house with a painter's disciplined eye. As a result, the rooms resonate with strong, almost dissonant, colors; layers of exotic fabrics; and eclectic, exotic, and over-scaled furnishings.

Hudson has created a home where the public spaces are distinct from the private ones, and where the most intimate spaces are the most revealing of personality and desire. Both Annie's and Genevieve's rooms capture different dream states—one, a tented Moroccan fantasy, the other, an imperious Chinese chamber. The master bedroom has been filled with family heirlooms and mementos of the couple's travels that will become their children's heirlooms.

Hudson's disregard for doctrinaire decorating displays itself in every detail. Her 38-foot-long living room glows under a turquoise ceiling. A collection of over-scaled pieces and exotic textiles quells the room's expansive dimensions. In the combined library/dining room, which overlooks the garden, she introduces the lightness of being in Thonet tubular copper chairs from the 1930s. With an eye for the painterly effect, this artist has decided to keep the unfinished stucco surfaces of partially stripped walls in the living room and stairwell, along with the remnants of a trompe l'oeil wallpaper border by the stairs.

ABOVE: Julian Schnabel suggested the blue concrete stairway that connects the patio to the house. The bronze-and-steel railing is by Studio 40. Schnabel also added leftover tiles from the bathroom renovation to the stone patio. The antique carved-wood chair is Moroccan. **RIGHT:** To make Annie's Moroccan fantasy bedroom, the late artist Ricky Clifton glued colored paper to the walls and ceiling with wheat paste and then glazed them with Mop & Glo. He also made woodblock prints for the borders. Vahakn Arslanian, a young artist, constructed the stained glass window.

ABOVE: David Zadeh of Symourgh International Inc., a New York company that specializes in antique Oriental and European rugs, collected eight antique Persian kilims, each 2 ½ feet wide and 12 to 20 feet long and similar in color and pattern. Zadeh then had them pieced together to create the runners that cover the stairs connecting the house's four floors. BELOW: In the living room, one of Hudson's paintings hangs above a chaise draped with early-nineteenth-century French and Spanish embroidered textiles. Tribeca Upholstery made the velvet pillows. When Hudson saw the pink primer on the walls with the plaster showing through, she decided to leave it as the final coat.

Skateboarder Genevieve Hudson-Price hangs out on the living room sofa. The room is filled with Indian, Chinese, and Indian pieces. Hudson created pattern with layer upon layer of Eastern and ethnic textiles. The stucco-like effect on the walls was created by Jean François Aimé, an expert plasterer, who treated them with a roughly applied mixture of powdered and liquid pigment and plaster.

ABOVE: The 38-foot-long living room is anchored with a spectacular double English sofa. Other overscaled furnishings include a red Chinese wedding chest, a carved-wood Indian bed that serves as a coffee table, and well-worn leather club chairs. "I have a catalog in my brain," says Hudson, who focuses on design even when watching TV. "*Brideshead Revisited* inspired the color of the ceiling," she says of the deep turquoise that gives the room its special lift. **LEFT:** The master bedroom contains a riot of pattern. A Morrocan caftan, Indian elephant headress, and Bokhara textiles drape the four-poster tiger-maple bed that once belonged to Hudson's parents. Tibetan tiger- and leopard-patterned rugs are on the floor. The nineteenth-century Philippine textile used as a bedspread comes from Tucker Robbins, New York.

THE MUSICIAN

Lorraine Kirke, the wife of rock musician Simon Kirke, shows what temperament has over training when it comes to creating interiors that express imagination. In the family's 120-year-old, 14-bedroom Shingle-style Hamptons house, color reigns, paint peels, sconces are mismatched, and only a few windows remain undraped.

With architect Sarah Calkins and builder Bob Plumb, Kirke reconfigured

the house to meet the needs of her family. They made a master suite out of four second-floor rooms, and added a large terrace and sleeping porch. They also built Simon a studio, and tore down the garage and put up a barn for the kids' music room. Then Kirke, a tireless shopper, began trolling the Hamptons's antiques stores, yard sales, and flea markets, Brooklyn's Atlantic Avenue, and her native London. She says, "I pick things up and never worry where I'll put them. If I like it, I'll find a place for it. That's what I think makes this a home."

But Kirke's real weakness is for architectural fragments. Cornices, pilasters, leaded-glass over doors, carved moldings call out to her. She adopts them, incorporating them into her houses as fanciful bed frames, as light filters and room dividers, or just as delightful ornament. The most pleasure often comes from the greatest challenge, like mounting a huge, fragile, open-work wood pediment over the second-floor terrace when her builder balked at the project.

Yet the two found a solution. After all, she explains, "I always think to myself, 'The Taj Mahal managed to get built. Why make a big deal out of these things.'"

OPPOSITE: Florals and stripes unite happily in the Kirkes' living room. The wood-frame armchairs are from Ruby Beets, Bridgehampton, NY; the wicker armchair and candleholders on the mantel are from the Yard Couple; the slipcover on the wing chair was made from fabric Kirke found in London. The paintings are, from left, by artist Michelle Dovey, a family friend, Domino Kirke, and Jemima Kirke. BELOW: Kirke's assured eye and imagination ensure that color and texture reign in rooms where sofas are piled with pillows, and tables are draped with quirky fabrics. As she says, "If it's perfect, it's boring."

ABOVE: Kirke, a tireless shopper, tends to see the less obvious beauty in things. "If it appeals to the eye, I get it," she says. Then she finds a place for it. Nothing reveals this free-spirited approach more clearly than the sink and bathtub, from Keystone in Hudson, NY, set out in the open in the master bedroom. The wing chairs, from England, are covered in white cotton canvas; the bed coverlet and mirrors are from Ruby Beets Antiques, Bridgehampton, NY. The folding screen is from Gray Gardens. **OPPOSITE TOP:** In the house's turret, Kirke has made a painting studio for her daughters. The room is outfitted with wood-framed windows that open to the panoramic views. **OPPOSITE BELOW:** Kirke has made a house that welcomes all kinds of creative activities, including making music, which her kids do. "The more space you give them," she says, "the longer they stay around."

THE FILMMAKER

Albert and Gillian Maysles's island summer house is redolent with memories and literary history. Legend has it that the daughters of Mr. Fox, the former owner of the island who built the 18-room house in 1870, were members of William James's group of experimenters in the occult. Before the Maysleses' occupation, the house provided a setting for Robert Rushmore's novella, *Open Water*, and a landscape for Sylvia Wright's *A Shark-Infested Rice Pudding*. Its nickname, Haunted House, is entirely appropriate, especially when you remember that Albert and his late brother, David, made *Grey Gardens,* the 1976 documentary about two destitute relatives of Jacqueline Onassis and their decrepit East Hampton mansion.

Gillian's father, John Walker, former director of the National Gallery of Art, bought the house in 1967 to preserve the family tradition of island summers. Gillian insists that the place "has a way of demanding more serious pursuits than golf or tennis," and that it inspired her father to complete books on Whistler and Turner, and Bruce Chatwin to begin *In Patagonia,* and has prompted the artistic tendencies of her three children.

Over the past 33 years, the Maysleses have made the house the place where the different generations reconnect. Gillian calls it "our collection of memories. I wanted it to look as it might have in the nineteenth century." That means, among other things, no TV and a dining room frequently bathed in candlelight. Some rooms still have the original wall frescoes in the colors of Pompeii and Herculaneum. One significant concession to the future is architect Jim Righter's addition: children's rooms modeled on the Pullman sleeper cars that delighted Gillian as a child.

ABOVE: Not much has changed in the Maysleses' summer house since it was built by Mr. Fox in the 1870s. John Walker, Gillian Maysles's father, the long-time director of the National Gallery of Art, found it particularly appealing because it faces west, toward the sunset. The front hall has its original Pompeiian red walls. The prints in the stairwell have been added. **OPPOSITE:** The Maysleses rarely use electric lighting in the dining room, preferring silver candlesticks on the tables and Georgian candelabras on the sideboard. Old prints of Rome, including one that is backlighted, hang on the dining room wall.

BELOW: The family doesn't have a television set, so adults and children amuse themselves with reading, writing, and drawing in its memento-filled rooms. The house came with rooms full of painted furniture, and, it is said, a ghost. "Legend has it," says Gillian, "that Fox's daughters were friends of William James's and participated in his experiments in the occult, which is why the house was always considered haunted." **RIGHT:** Gillian's father wrote books on Whistler and Turner in this room. Gillian says, "The house has its calm way of demanding more serious pursuits than golf and tennis." The place seems to inspire creativity, particularly in writers, like Bruce Chatwin, who have visited, or those, like Robert Rushmore or Sylvia Wright, who have lived there.

When the Maysleses began adapting the house to suit their own way of life and family, Gillian insisted on keeping the kitchen pretty much the way it had always been. Only the Art Nouveau tiles, the William Morris curtain fabric from Sanderson, and the Viking range have been added. The soapstone sink and mismatched china came with the house.

ABOVE: Gillian says she likes "raggle-taggle" decorating. In the master bedroom, she combined a nineteenth-century American bed with an antique gateleg table she inherited from her grandmother. The Chinese rug happened to match the frescoed walls. Prints of the Zodiac line the wall above the bed.

RIGHT: Because Gillian loved sleeping in Pullman berths as a girl, when she was planning an addition to the house, she asked Boston architect Jim Righter to design "berths" in the wall for her children. Now the three girls each have a sleeping space with a bookshelf and a light. Two of the ceilings are painted with sky and stars, a third is colored a dark red. The berths line the balcony overlooking a double-height room painted Venetian pink. **OPPOSITE ABOVE AND BELOW:** Some of the rooms in the house retained their original frescoed walls in the original colors, while others were painted in similarly rich hues. While the house came with furniture-filled rooms, Gillian has slowly added to what there was. "The idea is to make the house as imaginary a place as possible," she explains. It's certainly filled with imagination, since she, her husband, and their three children are all artists.

THE DESIGNER

ABOVE: Shore's personal vision begins at the front door of her Georgian house. She has painted the door chalkboard black, and uses it as a surface for intricate chalk drawings that she redraws as they fade or wash away.

OPPOSITE: "Everything I do seems to have a story," Shore says. "It's all about finding things and putting them together." And, it seems, it's also about realizing, and then sharing, the fantasy, as she has in her interior garden. An antique mirror, a crystal chandelier, and arrangements of baskets and shells join palms, lilies, and gardenias in this extremely personal space.

When fashion stylist and designer Ann Shore moved to an early-Georgian house in the Spitalfields section of East London, she did so partly because the neighborhood had become one of the city's most vibrant artistic communities. In her house there, where past meets present in shaping the future, Shore has worked some powerful style magic to achieve what she terms "that global thing that's happening—a mix of everything that only the English, who have been branded with being quite eccentric, can do."

York stone floors, well-scrubbed boards with traces of centuries-old paint, and whitewashed walls set a rustic stage for a sophisticated sensibility that revels in the impromptu mix. Shore's small kitchen opens around the proverbial hearth—a coal-fired Aga stove that also heats the house. A vintage Royal Doulton sink abuts an elm drainboard used for storing the basic eating utensils. A York stone shelf above supports two banana leaves, dried in natural arabesques. Old wicker baskets nest haphazardly under the counter.

With a visual sense that revels in the contrast of ethereal and earthy, Shore has choreographed a bipolar interior landscape that swings between the delicate and rough, the consciously pretty and the honestly ugly, delighting in the differences. "I think of the raw, unpolished, and organic feel of the house as being balanced by a decorative daintiness," she says. She cultivates this contrast throughout the house, from an indoor garden that flourishes with exotic blooms nestled among shells and pearls to a bedroom draped with silk and sequins, with a mattress on the floor.

ABOVE: In the living room, she has grouped white linen pillows on an English leather armchair, along with an African mat and bowl, beads, a mud pot from Afghanistan, and an English oak mirror. **TOP LEFT:** In one corner of her studio, Shore has a Jacobsen Swan chair alongside an antique slip and a Balinese rucksack. **CENTER LEFT:** "I think of the raw, unpolished, and organic feel of the house as being balanced by decorative daintiness," Shore says. "It's a combination of masculine and feminine." That contrast is immediately clear in the bedroom, where Shore leaves the mattress on the wide-plank wood floor. A sequined throw and silk hangings, as well as cascading strands of necklaces add delicate, filigreed details to the room. **BELOW LEFT:** Shore describes her approach as "that global thing that's happening—a mix of everything that only the English, who have been branded with being quite eccentric, can do." Eccentricity reigns in the bathroom, which incorporates a French antique double-sided copper tub, filled by a hose from the sink, and a rusted water tank for the toilet that was rescued from a neighbor's outhouse. "They couldn't wait to get rid of it," remembers Shore. "They thought of us as poor, poor things." **OPPOSITE:** Shell, pearl, and crystal necklaces add to the allure of the bedroom.

ABOVE: The small kitchen combines rusticity and sophistication. Banana leaves on a York stone shelf rest above the old Royal Doulton sink. Shore stows her basic white ceramics and Duralex glasses on an elm drainboard. Unlike the old floor boards elsewhere, the kitchen has floors of York stone. She describes the space as "very basic." It is focused around a coal-fired Aga stove that is used for cooking all year round and to heat the house in winter. **OPPOSITE:** "I covered the refrigerator with a collage of black-and-white images," says Shore, "instead of having it sit there as a big white blob. Old wicker baskets are stacked helter-skelter under the counter.

ABOVE: Shore seems to have the gift of making soul-satisfying assemblages with whatever comes to hand. In the dining room, she has artfully stacked a collection of ash, oak, and cherry logs against the wall on either side of the fireplace. Food platters from Afghanistan sit on the long, rough-hewn table. **RIGHT:** In Shore's house, even basic white ceramic tableware and Duralex glasses drying casually on the elm drainboard look like a thoughtfully arranged domestic still life. **OPPOSITE:** A rubber plant winds up the stairway of the 1870s house. Hanging on the walls beside it are antique and ethnic fabrics. Shore takes care of the details effortlessly. "Although they might look complicated, to me they are part of having a total vision," she says. "A lot of people say it's an old-fashioned way of living, but to me it's very modern, because it's much simpler, and it all comes naturally."

GRAND TOUR

When decoration becomes a way to remember things past, the decorator seeks objects that, like Proust's madeleine, trigger memory on a grand scale.

A MOVABLE FEAST

A SENTIMENTAL EDUCATION

TOUR DE FRANCE

GIFTS FROM THE GREEKS

Decorating is hunting and gathering. In Grand Tour style, the quarry is civilization and its contents.

The walkabout, the odyssey, the road trip have always been rites of passage. But the grand tour proper dates from the eighteenth century, when the sun was still rising on the British Empire. No English gentleman's education—and, later, as economies and empires permitted, no Frenchman's, German's, Russian's, or American's—was complete without a survey of the world's great cities and sites. In the nineteenth century, John Ruskin, among others, championed the role of travel for the aesthete. In the twentieth, Bernard Berenson made connoisseurship a profession, advising international art dealer Lord Joseph Duveen.

The effects that humanity's greatest achievements have on us may fade in time, and in anticipation of that we often wish to bring some memento of them home. This acquisitive urge has its apotheosis in the world's great houses and museums, but also in the Grand Tour style of less well-known travelers whose rooms are much more than the sum of their souvenirs. These are people whose domestic style celebrates the passions, and obsessions, that drive human culture. And there are no accidental tourists.

OPPOSITE: John Knott's antelope horns, and marble Mars suggest places to go and stories to know.

A MOVABLE FEAST

Deep in the soul of many a collector is the desire to regain the empire lost, as a visit to the Paris apartment of French lawyer Jean-Luc Gauzere reveals. Gauzere, who represents museums and private clients, is himself an exuberant gatherer in the great French tradition. His apartment near the Louvre shows an appetite trained, like that of Napoleon's Louvre organizer, Dominique Vivant Denon, to savor living intimately with things.

Denon's private museum, his house, included a mummy's foot pocketed in Egypt, bits of the bones of Héloïse and Abelard, a piece of King Henry IV's mustache, and one of Voltaire's teeth. Gauzere's obsession and his home radiate a similar passion for things rich in historical associations: chairs made for the Duc D'Otrante, one of Napoleon's ministers; an embroidered portfolio made for the Duchesse de Berry; a silver chalice made for "Mad" King Ludwig of Bavaria. Gauzere lives in the ultimate bachelor apartment—sans children's rooms, guest room, dining room—in a building dating from 1810, when much of Europe was France's accumulation.

Gauzere credits his love of sumptuousness, and his distaste for careful decoration, to the period of his childhood spent in a Saharan oasis town. "I'm never afraid to go too far," he says. "I love Rothschild taste." A phenomenon of the Napoleon III era, Rothschild taste— that is, a gift for making sensuous, operatic acquisitions—in Gauzere's case extends to mementos from empires ranging from Tutankhamen to the Romanoffs.

When Gauzere gives dinner parties, he sets up the table wherever he wants. When he eats alone, it seems he's also surrounded by companions, because his objects relate the spirited gossip of other eras.

OPPOSITE: Dominating the living room is a silver-leafed nineteenth-century table, once owned by the maharana of Udaipur, where Gauzere displays his so-called "playthings"—including silver models of ships and temples—many made for Indian nobility. **BELOW:** The room also contains two red velvet-covered, early-nineteenth-century Indian silver thrones.

TOP: Gauzere's love for an extremely sensuous, operatic kind of decor translates into an aesthetic he terms "Rothschild taste," a phenomenon with historical roots in the Napoleon III era that reappears here in the red upholstered walls of the salon. **ABOVE RIGHT:** The green moiré silk walls of the living room and overstuffed chairs with red damask-patterned upholstery also suggest Napoleon III. **ABOVE LEFT:** A nineteenth-century bust of Czar Peter the Great broods over the salon, set up for dining with chairs made for the Duc d'Otrante, one of Napoleon's ministers.

OPPOSITE: A view through the enfilade of rooms gives the barest overview of Gauzere's collections, which he amassed through every-other-day trips to the auction rooms at the Hotel Drouot. High points include an embossed silver chalice made for "Mad" King Ludwig of Bavaria, an ivory model of King Tutankhamen's tomb, a trove of Indian portraits, a set of gilded Romanoff arms, and all sorts of mementos of French nobility.

Gauzere credits a childhood in a Saharan oasis town for his love of exuberance, which he expresses in the master bedroom with a silver embroidered velvet bedcover from Pakistan.

A SENTIMENTAL EDUCATION

"Life is too short," says Libby Holsten. "I deal in superlatives." An antiques dealer and designer, the Newport, Rhode Island–based Holsten harnesses the collector's passion to a sense of place. She imposes her will to the last detail, as her 3,300-square-foot, two-bedroom apartment in a 100-year-old Newport house attests. Holsten's place—with 14-foot ceilings, French doors, terrace, and views of water on two sides—contains a lovingly assembled lesson in the history of European decorative arts from the sixteenth through the early nineteenth centuries.

"I love things as they are, and I like them to look old, untouched, unrestored—like they've been that way always," Holsten says. She likes to mix the mundane with the elegant, the large with the small, the precious with the not. She has a particular fondness for painted furniture from all periods, as well as a taste for a muted palette of whites, creams, and beiges (as well as Swedish blue and a hint of mauve) designed to show her favorites at their best.

"Two rooms are Swedish, one is Biedermeier, and one is French," Holsten says. "Going from room to room is like going from country to country." An armchair traveler who hates to fly, she has assembled her remarkable collection using an indomitable spirit, a trusted network of contacts, and travel-happy friends willing to check on possibilities in faraway places. It is up to her to connect the global dots.

ABOVE: Holsten's Biedermeier room includes a Biedermeier lyre-base table and lyre-back chairs from the 1820s, a Biedermeier pier glass, and a Biedermeier settee. The harp is eighteenth-century Italian. The 1820s clock over the fireplace is Austrian. The French armoire is made of cherry. The eighteenth-century Swedish chandelier is paint and gilt. The antiquities resting on the fireplace mantel are first- and second-century Greek and Roman vessels. Pewter chargers hang over each doorway. **OPPOSITE:** The Biedermeier room also contains an antique Peking Chinese rug, a Dutch kas, a bass fiddle, and an eighteenth-century French tole tulipière atop a Biedermeier table.

OPPOSITE TOP: The main salon includes a 12-panel eighteenth-century coromandel screen, an eighteenth-century Italian gilt-wood chandelier, an eighteenth-century Italian marble-topped paint-and-gilt table once in the collection of Eleanor McMillen, a signed eighteenth-century chair, eighteenth-century French scales, and a French marble putto from the early or mid-nineteenth century. **OPPOSITE BOTTOM:** Another view of the Biedermeier room shows the range of Holsten's interests. **ABOVE:** The sitting room/bedroom features a bluestone floor, an 1820s Austrian chandelier, an eighteenth-century Russian chair, a pair of nineteenth-century Scandinavian chairs, a rare Swedish desk with an attached clock, and a late eighteenth-century French daybed and corona. The bookstand is Italian, the putti, French. Holsten's palette of subtle neutral shades shows off the fine lines of the furnishings.

ABOVE: Although Holsten specializes in furniture from the eighteenth and nineteenth centuries, she also collects instruments, antiquities, and tableware. In the bedroom/sitting room, she mounted a plate rack over the late-eighteenth/early-nineteenth Scandinavian settee to house a collection of plates and ephemera that includes eighteenth-century pewter chargers and chestnut urns, Creamware, four seventeenth-century faience lions, and Wedgwood white-and-gold dishes.
OPPOSITE: Among the prizes of Holsten's porcelain holdings is a set of unmarked early Sèvres.

TOUR DE FRANCE

When some people go home at night, they want to be transported to a different time and place. John S. Knott, president of Quadrille Wallpapers and Fabrics, is such a person, as his sultry, sensuously decorated one-bedroom apartment in New York makes clear. In Knott's case, the place to be is Paris, in the nineteenth century. He has used warm, burnished colors, uplighting, and an eclectic mix of neoclassical furnishings to create the after-hours atmosphere of the City of Light. And, like some women—say those in a novel by Colette—his rooms virtually glow in the dark.

When Knott first saw this apartment, it was a wreck—a shattered beauty with great bones—distinguished by high ceilings and a bay window. But stripping the woodwork revealed the original, African mahogany moldings. Knott had painter Julius Zsikla lacquer the walls in a color he calls saddle leather, a hue inspired by an Hermès appointment book.

The painted walls, says Knott, powerfully suggest the presence of the past, creating a luminous backdrop for a collection of things that would make any nineteenth-century globe-trotter feel at home and ready for tea.

Fin de siècle interiors are celebrated for their element of surprise and delight, and Knott's homage is no different. He has carefully calculated the play of color and pattern—the geometrics of a pair of gilded-bronze Japanese drum tables atop multicolored herringbone coco matting, for example—and the introduction of the unexpected. An elaborate eighteenth-century Venetian console table supports a huge contemporary flowerlike painting. The effect is monolithic, and modern, until the eye realizes that the painting's surface consists of densely scripted writings from the Rosetta stone.

LEFT: Knott's living room tends to the neoclassical, with walls lacquered a terra-cotta orange to match an Hermès appointment book, and multicolored herringbone coco matting from Carpet Innovations providing a background for a marvelous collection of eighteenth-, nineteenth-, and twentieth-century furniture and objects.
OPPOSITE: The living room desk acts as a convenient display surface for some of Knott's Grand Tour souvenirs.

The lacquered walls offer a glossy backdrop for a brown-leather-covered George III gilded settee and two 1940s Louis XVI-style slipper chairs with Russian leather upholstery. Accent pillows in Cosimo fabric by Quadrille, New York, gilded-bronze Japanese drum tables, and the floor matting add pattern. Antelope horns from John Roselli International, a bust of Mars, and a pair of nineteenth-century urns enrich the mix.

ABOVE: Knott bisected his classically proportioned living room with a sofa clad in Courtesan, a satin-and-chenille damask from Quadrille. A tole chandelier hangs over the sofa, which is backed by a nineteenth-century mechanical table from Pagoda in Hudson, NY. The neoclassical armchairs are from Arenskjold Art in Hudson. A silk tiger fabric on an ottoman and a Tramp art wooden pyramid add hints of exoticism. **LEFT:** Eclectic furnishings in the living room include an eighteenth-century gilded console, a modestly clad nineteenth-century plaster torso, a Moroccan wall sconce, and an Asian lacquered box from Pagoda. The large, contemporary flowerlike painting by Simrel Achenbach is actually an image of the Rosetta stone's densely scripted surfaces. **OPPOSITE:** The table at the living room's bay window is covered in a damask from Quadrille.

ABOVE: The Grand Tour theme continues in Knott's bedroom. The room is enveloped in Turkestan fabric from Quadrille, which has the same range of colors as the coco matting on the floor. Blue-green is the complement of orange, and its appearance as an accent reinforces the mood of the rooms. A collection of nineteenth-century engravings of decorative details hangs on the upholstered walls. **OPPOSITE:** A nineteenth-century American Phyfe & Sons sleigh bed from Frank & Jacqueline Donegan Antiques in Hudson, NY, is dressed in La Scala and Shangri-la, both from Quadrille.

GIFTS FROM
THE GREEKS

When a reading of Gibbon's *Decline and Fall of the Roman Empire* inspires the first acquisition of a now notable collection of antiquities, that old saw about Greeks and gifts takes on new meaning. Gibbon, and the ensuing passion for everything ancient, launched this couple on a personal design odyssey that has resulted in the transformation of a classic ranch house into a Doric-style retreat. Designed by the New York–based partnership of Patrick Naggar and Terese Carpenter, the quasi-temple along the border between New York and Connecticut offers a paean to a high cultural ideal. As the wife observes, "Why not re-create one of humanity's best moments? The thing about being American is that your past doesn't have to have anything to do with your present."

The Beaux Arts–trained Naggar set the house between the trees. Reminiscent of the Parthenon, the porticoed structure with fluted Doric columns has a symmetrical floor plan, a triangulated pediment, and a dentil-ornamented cornice. "I wanted to reset all the clocks in this period of stylistic confusion," says Naggar. "There is an important American tradition of the neoclassical, but I wanted to go further, to the Doric, the least ornamented and so most modern of the classical orders of architecture. It was an exercise in style, combining the monumental and the domestic."

The interior owes a similar debt to the ancients, down to the last detail. "Every part of the interior relates to antiquity," says Carpenter, "from the doorknobs, which are Mycenaean in design, to the thickness of the doors, which are as we imagined ancient Greek doors to have been."

From the French Aubusson carpet to the frescoes, nature pervades the living room. The curtains are Rogers & Goffigon's Edelweiss. The French bronze and alabaster chandelier and the Liberty Thebes chairs are late nineteenth century. Clarence House's Velours Gatinais covers the sofas. The 1920s Swedish console, by Folke Bensow, supports an Attic vase from 470 B.C. Atop the fireplace are two Wedgwood terra-cotta vases and a black Mesopotamian beaker.

ABOVE: "The Victory of Alexander," a nineteenth-century plaster frieze, winds around the sitting room. The curtains are from Chelsea Editions. A nineteenth-century Greek-style amphora stands on a 1927 lacquer table by Einar Hjort. The sofa fabrics include Brunschwig & Fils's Scala Metisse and Fonthill's Agora. Brunschwig & Fils's Bentley Ticking covers the campaign chair. The Chinese sea-grass carpet is from Stark. LEFT: Naggar domesticated the facade's Doric elements by using cedar. OPPOSITE: The master bedroom contains a world of treasures, including a third-century A.D. Roman column from Ariadne Galleries, NYC, a nineteenth-century French bronze-and-leather reclining bed, and a nineteenth-century bust. The Louis XVI limestone mantel is from 1760. The seventeenth-century cabinet is Chinese. The reproduction Fortuny silk ceiling fixture is from Odegard. Bergamo's Marquis covers the sofa.

ABOVE LEFT: A limestone bathtub dominates a pale-blue and limestone master bathroom. The hardware on the French doors and the plumbing fixtures are from P.E. Guerin. The curtains are Rogers & Goffigon's Matisse Summer. The space also includes a custom slate mantel, marble sink, and nineteenth-century bronze and alabaster hanging light. **ABOVE RIGHT:** The guest bedrooms also open onto the garden. **OPPOSITE:** Naggar says, "The master bedroom was to be a sort of Marco Polo room, a traveler's den." Hanging from the coffered ceiling is a reproduction Fortuny silk pendant light from Odegard. A nineteenth-century Neapolitan steel bed from Ariane Dandois, a Parisian antiques dealer, dominates the room; entwined serpents and a Greek key motif detail the headboard. The burgundy silk-and-linen damask curtains are in Rubelli Mocenigo by Bergamo, with under curtains by Rogers & Goffigon.

MID-CENTURY MODERN

In the golden age of design, when there are problems, there are solutions, and when there are questions, there are always many answers.

FIFTIES AND FABULOUS

LET IT BE

A REVERENCE FOR WOOD

THE WRIGHT WAY

ALL IN THE FAMILY

Let's hop on pop. Pop culture, that is. Mid-century-Modern style is back. And it's more universal, and sexier, than the first time.

That's as it should be. Remember that the stuff of mid-century modern was conceived with a democratic attitude. After World War II, every man, everywhere, needed affordable housing and furniture. The young turks of American design—the Eameses, George Nelson, Isamu Noguchi, Harry Bertoia, Eero Saarinen—and others, elsewhere, answered the call for a brave new world with good design that could roll off the assembly line.

The evolution of modernism may lie somewhere between Dessau and Detroit, between the Bauhaus and Cranbrook. Less is more? As R. Buckminster Fuller said, do more with less. Consider the mid-century modernists the second generation, the graduates who took the modernist show on the road. And, yes, they also did incredible things with plastics—from the linear to the squiggly, from the amoebic to the atomic.

Maybe hindsight is twenty-twenty. But this renaissance is more than mere nostalgia. Today's conditions? Youthquake, new economy, global renaissance, industrial revolution. Today's solutions? Re-create the world in a mid-century modern image, one that's populist, luminous, economical, witty, efficient, safe, and intelligent.

OPPOSITE: Lawrence and Sharon Tarantino have righted Wright, restoring the missing pieces to their Usonian house.

FIFTIES AND FABULOUS

What Atlanta-based interior designer William Stewart collects, he collects with a passion. These days, the objects of his considerable affection are mid-century American and European designs, the ones he calls the "greatest hits of the recent past." Not only has he pursued his vintage finds assiduously, he has settled them into a proper home, a single-story, 2,700-square-foot modern house in the city's Buckhead section, where the preferred style is more Tara than Taliesen. His house was designed in 1951 by Jeffrey McConnell, a Georgia Tech graduate who was, Stewart says, "a bit of a rebel. The house shows the influence of Frank Lloyd Wright, Schindler, and Neutra."

The place needed work before Stewart and his family could move in. The renovation included painted metals, hardwood and stone floors, and a flexible furniture plan. "I soon realized that I wanted to live very simply," he explains, "and all of a sudden the words 'natural materials' meant something to me."

Stewart's catalog of designers ranges from Charlotte Pérriand and Jean Prouvé, George Nelson, Russel Wright, George Nakashima, and Charles and Ray Eames to Eva Zeisel, Serge Mouille, and Mathieu Matagot. He even embraces contemporary designers, among them Ralph Lauren, Stefano Giovannoni, and Jasper Morrison. He adds, "We don't live in the past, so I didn't want the house to be terribly serious. I want to have a good time and I want people who come here to have a good time. This furniture has a history, and we're only caretakers for a short period."

ABOVE: Jean Royère's 1950 Tree lamp decorates the den, where the furniture is arranged for television viewing. The three-legged tables are by George Nakashima, as are the wood chairs upholstered in an Osborne & Little fabric. The leather sofa is by Jasper Morrison for Cappellini. **RIGHT:** In the living room, designs by Jean Prouvé (two chairs in the foreground), Mathieu Mategot (metal side table), Charlotte Pérriand and Prouvé (coffee table), and Eva Zeisel (bowl) coexist with Jasper Morrison's poufs.

TOP: Stewart has assembled designs that he calls "the greatest hits of the recent past." The A-list in his master bedroom includes Eero Saarinen's pedestal table, Womb chair, and ottoman for Knoll, and George Nelson's Slat Bench for Herman Miller. **ABOVE:** As Stewart says, "Modern may not be down-stuffed, but it's still comfortable." **ABOVE RIGHT:** Designed in 1951 by Georgia Tech alumnus Jeffrey McConnell, the one-story house is one of the first modern houses in Atlanta's Buckhead district. **OPPOSITE:** Tin robots stand guard off the foyer, where two 1953 Frank Lloyd Wright plywood chairs sit under a 1950s clock by George Nelson for the Howard Miller Clock Company.

ABOVE: Stewart designed the master bathroom's two checkerboard patterns with tiles from Dal Tile. The photograph is by Len Prince. A Herman Miller chair by Charles and Ray Eames sits by the bathtub. RIGHT: In the guest bedroom, the two Eames 1946 LCWS chairs serve as nightstands. The 1958 Philco Predicta television has been retrofitted for cable. The photograph over the bed is *Milk Cross* by Andres Serrano.

LET IT BE

When Nanette and Eric Brill started searching for their dream house, they had more than just a vague idea of modern in mind. They wanted "a contemporary house in original condition," specifically a sleek house in Bedford Hills, New York, that Edward Durell Stone had designed in 1933 for Richard H. Mandel, with interiors by Donald Deskey. From the ceremonial stairs in the unusual, glass-fronted foyer to the spectacular curved wall in the dining room, the house is a rare example of early American modernist architecture in its purest form.

Although allowed to deteriorate, the house itself had not been modified over the years; the floor plan was intact, and many of the original materials and details remained. The Brills negotiated to keep the furniture that Deskey designed specifically for the house—about 65 pieces in all. To supplement the existing pieces, the Brills have collected other Deskey designs from the same period.

The project has proved to be as much a treasure hunt as a restoration drama. Old photographs have been useful in the slow process of putting the rooms back together and identifying long-stored items of furniture. The Brills consider themselves "caretakers rather than owners." They never fail to appreciate the house's stark spaces and the way round forms play against straight lines—a combination influenced by the Russian Constructivists and International Style, which defined modern architecture for a good portion of this century. As Eric says, "Our love of this place is not nostalgic. It works very well as a place for living. We see it as architecture that looks to the future."

OPPOSITE: The sofas, side chairs, ashtray stand, coffee table, and standing lamps are all Donald Deskey designs that date from around 1929. **ABOVE:** Calling themselves caretakers rather than owners, Eric and Nannette Brill have taken very few liberties in their restoration of the house. They are in the process of replacing the original half-inch-thick cork tile floors in the living room, and, to honor Stone and Deskey's original plans, have added a floor-to-ceiling expanse of mirror around the plain-fronted fireplace. The aluminum andirons are by Deskey. A 1935 photograph from *A/Z*, a German magazine, is framed in burl wood,

ABOVE: Committed modernists, the Brills have long collected contemporary art. LEFT: The Brills purchased their American modernist dream house, designed by Edward Durell Stone and Donald Deskey for Richard H. Mandel in the early 1930s, along with about 65 pieces of the furniture originally created for it. When they took possession, the roof needed replacing, dozens of casement windows and plaster windowsills required scraping and painting, and the dining room's curved-glass-block wall, a counterpoint to the straight lines of windows and terraces, demanded attention. The house had been well-documented, which helped in the restoration.

The glass-block-enclosed foyer, with its high cement planter, looks much as it did when the house was built more than 60 years ago. The ceremonial staircase has a Deskey-designed, one-of-a-kind polished aluminum railing.

ABOVE: In addition to the stair rail, other Deskeyisms that survived the years intact include the overscale stainless-steel kitchen and pantry sinks, with wavy dividers, and a huge circular mirror in the ground-floor powder room. **OPPOSITE:** The dining room, with a curved-glass-block wall and black terrazzo floor, is one of the house's most distinctive and dramatic spaces. Deskey made the one-of-a-kind Bakelite dining table, which has an illuminated glass insert, specifically for the house. Putting the rooms back together was a slow but exciting process, and required intuition and patience, as well as the collectors' bloodhound instincts for nosing out and identifying long-stored pieces of furniture and appropriate alternatives when the originals were unavailable. The Brills added the Gilbert Rohde–designed green-leather-and-metal chairs. The grandfather clock by the wall is also from the 1930s.

A REVERENCE FOR WOOD

The late George Nakashima, a Japanese-American original, honored what he called "the soul of the tree." His furniture marries the ecstatic simplicity of the Shakers with the serenity of the Japanese. And, as Japanese custom dictates, he taught his eldest child, Mira Nakashima-Yarnall, herself an architect and furniture designer, who runs the business her father started 54 years ago.

Known primarily as a furniture maker, Nakashima was also an architect. He built, among other things, a remarkable house, called Sansō, or Mountain Villa, in Bucks County, Pennsylvania, that he left both to his family and to those who visit the region. Completed in 1978 and modeled on the summer homes of the Japanese bourgeoisie, Sansō is Nakashima's last and most traditional structure. In true Japanese style, the small space fuses formal and private life by serving many purposes. "This is where we have parties, tea ceremonies, Japanese-style baths—all the occasions we observe as a family," Nakashima-Yarnall says.

The compound also includes, across the road, a private building that Nakashima built in 1970. "It was a trick," says Mira, to lure her back as an apprentice and work mate. And it worked. Inspired by the Katsura Rikyū, the seventeenth-century imperial residence in Kyoto built partly on stilts, Nakashima set the front of the house on pylons and attached a gracefully bowing deck. The interior of the house celebrates the inner life of trees. But while lumber serves as the house's centerpiece, not everything is built of it. As Mira explains, "Dad had a theory that if the design is good enough, it doesn't matter what materials you use."

ABOVE: Nakashima used a variation of traditional Japanese sliding Shoji screens to divide rooms and provide a luminous backdrop for his furniture. A sofa bed, with its mountainous head of English oak burl, anchors the sitting area. **OPPOSITE:** The side table's delicate legs contrast with its rugged free-form burl top and the lamp's gnarly base. Nakashima designed the carved cabinet for the Odakyu department store in Tokyo.

ABOVE: The refurbished mahogany Steinway takes pride of place in the house Nakashima built for his daughter. The artist removed the varnish from the wood and rubbed it with oil to bring out the grain. **LEFT:** Nakashima's compound includes two houses. His, called Sansō, or the Mountain Villa, was completed in 1978. Modeled on the summer villas of Japanese bourgeoisie, it was the architect's last, and most traditional, building. The house he built for his daughter and her family, across the road, was inspired by Katsura Rikyū, in Tokyo, the celebrated seventeenth-century imperial residence built partly on stilts.
OPPOSITE: His dining room contains a table crafted of Persian walnut and eight Conoid chairs. Along one wall is a matching shelf and a print by the late Ben Shahn, a family friend.

BELOW: In true Japanese style, the Mountain Villa fuses formal and private life, serving many purposes elegantly. "This is where we have parties, tea ceremonies, Japanese-style baths—all the special occasions we observe as a family," says Nakashima-Yarnall. The boomerang shape of the Japanese bath is a Nakashima signature. The tub is decorated with designs by the artist's son, Kevin, and each of his grandchildren. Random-width floorboards are black walnut interspersed with bloody birch, a luminous, crimson timber. **RIGHT:** The tea room, with a floor covered in traditional tatami mats and Shojilike window panels, doubled as a Buddhist temple in 1997, when Zen master Eido Tai Shimano-Roshi performed Nakashima's seven-year memorial ceremony. The space honors nature, in Japanese fashion, and the refining touch of the hand. **BELOW RIGHT:** In Nakashima-Yarnall's house, the rooms are meant to celebrate the inner life of trees. The humbler elements serve as foils for a collection of Nakashima-designed treasures. Unfinished plywood walls, for example, set off hanging cabinets of lustrous cherry; elsewhere, vinyl flooring contrasts with stair railings of curly maple.

THE WRIGHT WAY

ABOVE: Wright designed all of the built-in seating, cabinets, shelving, tables, dining chairs, desks, beds, and lighting for his Usonian houses. Here, the built-ins and desks had survived. The Tarantinos repaired or reconstructed the rest using information on Wright's original plan or from the original owner. **OPPOSITE:** The furniture is constructed of Philippine mahogany. The clerestory panel designs are abstracted from the Samara, or winged seed of the pine tree.

Like many people, architect Lawrence Tarantino and his wife, designer Sharon Tarantino, have their dream house. Unlike most, theirs is by Frank Lloyd Wright. Known as the Bachman-Wilson house, the 1954 house near Princeton, New Jersey, is one of a series of relatively small, relatively inexpensive houses that Wright designed from the 1930s until his death in 1959. He called them Usonian, meaning American (and perhaps utopian).

The Tarantinos bought the 1,500-square-foot house in 1988. "It was a dream come true," says Lawrence, a Wright fan since his student days. Like other Usonian houses, this one follows the master's plan for a low structure with a solid, street-facing wall. The other facade consists of glass windows onto the backyard. The open interior is divided by a central utilities core, with snug perimeter spaces for bedrooms, hallways, and entrance. A cantilevered mezzanine adds more bedrooms and a balcony. A clerestory on three sides increases the light inside.

"Wright reduced everything as much as he could to save on building costs," Lawrence explains. He used simple materials—glass, concrete, and wood—in unusual ways, and designed built-in furniture, including seating, cabinets, desks, beds, shelving, tables, dining room chairs, and lighting. The Tarantinos refinished the elements that remained, and repaired or reconstructed other designs found on Wright's original plan or from Abe Wilson, the house's original owner. That, too, is part of the Usonian tradition. "It was a way to recycle and, at the same time, to be economical by using leftover pieces of wood whenever possible," says Lawrence. "Most owners of Usonian houses were handy people."

After all, it's part of the American dream.

ABOVE: Owning and maintaining a Wright-designed house requires an intrepid spirit, a real appreciation for history, and a clever set of hands. The Tarantinos have all three. In addition to the missing furniture, they renovated or restored the broken concrete terraces (above right), leaking roofs, rotted balconies (like the one outside the master bedroom above), moldy concrete exterior block walls, peeling urethane, and chipped layers of paint on the red concrete floors. They delved into the archives of the Frank Lloyd Wright Foundation and the Getty Institute, which hold Wright's drawings and letters, and completed the work according to the Secretary of the Interior's Standards for Rehabilitation, as well as the Restoration Guidelines from the Frank Lloyd Wright Building Conservancy. **OPPOSITE:** Wright's Usonian houses are celebrated for their elegant use of everyday materials and their efficient use of limited space, particularly in the kitchen, which the Tarantino's rebuilt to Wright's specifications, incorporating the laundry on the house's original plan. The Tarantinos say, "Every day living in the house offers an enriching experience and provides a spiritual appreciation of nature without ever leaving the house. We are living with a work of art, and we realize now Wright's genius more and more."

ALL IN THE FAMILY

Design is a communal effort. But sometimes it takes a project like the one that French mavericks Garouste & Bonetti and Martin Szekely have created for a family of four in Nouilly, France, to bring that fact home. The owners of this six-bedroom *hotel particulaire* from the late 1960s wanted an interior that suited the house's spirit. Although they collect modern art, and own some modern furniture, they weren't well versed in contemporary design. So they consulted a relative, an expert, Didier Krzentowski, who owns the Paris-based Gallery Kreo, which deals in design from the 1970s to the present. He suggested that Garouste & Bonetti and Martin Szekely do the place.

"The client wanted a comfortable, modern house," explains Mattia Bonetti. "They have some art, including a Warhol, and they wanted furniture that would fit." The design is based on a harmony of pale sycamore wood, iron with white gold leaf, and a shade of yellow more saturated than the sycamore, augmented by green and gray. Many of the pieces are unique to this residence.

About the collaboration with Szekely, Bonetti says, "We know each other well, and we knew what the other person was working on, but we didn't actually work together. To create a total look, we didn't want pieces that matched." They don't, except in spirit. A number of modernist and contemporary designers have been added to the mix, including Achille Castiglione, Ron Arad, Pucci di Rossi, Andrea Branzi, Ettore Sottsass, and Marc Newsom. Didier notes, "I wanted to use just the top furniture from the best designers of today from all countries." That's quite a community.

Garouste & Bonetti incorporated many of the clients'
existing pieces of furniture, such as these three sofas,
into the new interior that they and Martin Szekely
designed for this 1960s house in Nouilly, France. The
light-filled living room sings with bright colors and mod
forms. The copper coffee table is by Martin Szekely.

ABOVE: A dramatic stairwell framed in wood, designed by Martin Szekely, slices through the core of the house to the marble-lined foyer. A red-and-black throne by Pucci di Rossi sits at the base of the stairs. **ABOVE RIGHT:** Szekely also redesigned the foyer of the house, putting in a white marble floor and designing a white marble radiator grill and console. **OPPOSITE:** A custom-designed chandelier by Garouste & Bonetti hangs in the stairwell. The fixture, which is a rather narrow

cylinder about 15-feet high, drops through two stories. The design consists of a wrought-iron armature finished in white gold leaf and a white silk shade. Garouste & Bonetti also designed sconces made of the same materials to line the stairwell. Mattia Bonetti says, "The cylinder is simple, and geometric. The shape contrasts with the sharp, angular form of the stairs. It goes from the top of the house almost to the ground floor."

ABOVE: In this house, space flows freely between the living and dining rooms. A chandelier by Achille Castiglione hangs over the custom-designed dining table. **BELOW:** Every element of the interior has been carefully chosen or designed to suit the unique environment. **OPPOSITE:** Garouste & Bonetti developed a color palette for the interior that is based, says Bonetti, "on the harmony of pale wood, iron with white gold leaf, a soft yellow that goes with the sycamore wood, green and gray." In the living room, the Garouste & Bonetti-designed rug is made from a mixture of wool and raffia. Garouste & Bonetti also designed the sofas and the bronze-and-glass-topped table.

ABOVE: The dining room is both mod and modern. Martin Szekely designed the table with an unusual metal base. Garouste & Bonetti designed the gray silk-upholstered dining chairs specifically for this project. They have elegant, white-gold-finished sabots meant to work with the table legs.

OPPOSITE: Another Garouste & Bonetti design in the dining room is the Kawakubo chest of drawers, named after Japanese clothing designer Rei Kawakubo, which also has white-gold-finished hardware.

Garouste & Bonetti designed everything in the master bedroom specifically for this interior. The bed, chairs, bedside tables, lamps, cabinets, and curtains are all custom, and patterned upon simple, graphic, geometric forms that repeat from element to element. Here, they have extended the palette with shades of green and gray used in the bedcovers, curtains, and rug. "The gray," says Bonetti, "is meant to echo the white gold leaf used as an accent elsewhere in the house."

B Five Studio inset Italian Gubbio pottery in a macassar ebony-topped custom dining table.

RESOURCES

There is no style without shopping. Here's where to find what you've seen on these pages, and more.

UPDATED CLASSICS
PAGES 12–51

Featured Architects and Designers

Boris Baranovich Architects
153 Waverly Place
New York, NY 10014
212-627-1150

Brian McCarthy, Inc.
1414 Avenue of the Americas
Suite 1103
New York, NY 10019
212-308-7600

Francis Fleetwood, Architect
25 Newton Lane
East Hampton, NY 11937
316-324-4994

Glenn Gissler
36 East 22nd Street
New York, NY 10010
212-228-9880

* Through architects and designers

Keith Irvine
Irvine & Fleming Inc.
150 East 58th Street
New York, NY 10155
212-888-6000

Mark Hampton Inc.
654 Madison Avenue
New York, NY 10021
212-753-4110

Salvatore LaRosa
B Five Studio
160 Fifth Avenue
New York, NY 10011
212-255-7827

Zajac & Callahan Inc.
666 Greenwich Street
New York, NY 10014
212-741-1367

Accessories

Fendi
800-FENDI-NY

Goldfeder-Kahan Framing Group Ltd.
37 West 20th Street
New York, NY 10011
212-242-5310

Gunston Hall Museum Shop
800-811-6966

John Rosselli Int. *
523 East 73rd Street
New York, NY 10021
212-772-2137

Primavera Gallery
808 Madison Avenue
New York, NY 10021
212-288-1569

Portantina
895 Madison Avenue
New York, NY 10021
212-472-0636

Treasures & Trifles
409 Bleeker Street
New York, NY 10014
212-243-2723

Treillage
418 East 75th Street
New York, NY 10021
212-535-2288

Vincent Asta
1152 Second Avenue
New York, NY 10021
212-750-3364

Fabrics, Wall Coverings, Trimmings

Bergamo *
979 Third Avenue
New York, NY 10022
212-888-3333

Brunschwig & Fils *
979 Third Avenue
New York, NY 10022
212-838-7878

Fabrics, Wall Coverings, Trimmings

Christopher Norman *
979 Third Avenue
New York, NY 10022
212-644-4100

Clarence House *
211 East 58th Street
New York, NY 10022
212-752-2890, 800-632-0076

Colefax & Fowler Group *
979 Third Avenue
New York, NY 10022
212-753-4488

Coraggio Textiles *
979 Third Avenue
New York, NY 10022
212-758-9885, 800-624-2420

Cowtan & Tout *
979 Third Avenue
New York, NY 10022
212-647-6900

Decorators Walk *
979 Third Avenue
New York, NY 10022
212-319-7100

Dualoy Leather *
45 West 34th Street
New York, NY 10001
212-736-3360

Falotico Studios *
800-316-5106

Fortuny *
979 Third Avenue
New York, NY 10022
212-753-7153

Henry Cassen *
979 Third Avenue
New York, NY 10022
212-319-7100

Hermes Leather
45 West 34th Street
New York, NY 10001
212-947-1153, 800-441-4488

* Through architects and designers

Houles USA *
979 Third Avenue
New York, NY 10022
212-935-3900

Larsen Inc. *
through Cowtan & Tout
979 Third Avenue
New York, NY 10022
212-647-6900

Jim Thompson *
979 Third Avenue
New York, NY 10022
212-758-5357, 800-262-0336

Lee Jofa *
979 Third Avenue
New York, NY 10022
212-688-0444, 800-4LEEJOFA

Old World Weavers *
979 Third Avenue
New York, NY 10022
212-355-7186

Passementerie Inc. *
979 Third Avenue
New York, NY 10022
212-355-7600

Westgate Fabrics, Inc. *
(Payne Fabrics)
979 Third Avenue
New York, NY 10022
212-752-1960, 800-543-4322

Rose Cumming *
979 Third Avenue
New York, NY 10022
212-593-2060

Rogers & Goffigon *
979 Third Avenue
New York, NY 10022
212-888-3242

Scalamandré *
942 Third Avenue
New York, NY 10022
212-980-3888, 800-932-4361

Schumacher *
800-332-3384

Stroheim & Romann *
155 East 56th Street
New York, NY 10022
212-486-1500

Waterhouse Wallhangings *
260 Maple Street
Chelsea, MA 02150
617-423-7688

Zuber & Cie *
979 Third Avenue
New York, NY 10022
212-486-9226

Fittings, Fixtures, Hardware

Urban Archaeology
285 Lafayette Street
New York, NY 10012
212-431-6969

Joseph Biunno Ltd.
129 West 29th Street
New York, NY 10001
212-629-5630

Harrington Brassworks
7 Pearl Court
Allendale, NJ 07401
201-818-1300

Crown City Hardware Co.
800-950-1047

Fireplaces

Chesney's Fireplace Gallery *
979 Third Avenue
New York, NY 10022
646-840-0609

**Danny Alessandro, Ltd.,
Edwin Jackson, Inc.**
223 East 59th Street
New York, NY 10022
212-421-1928

Flooring

**Abraham Moheban & Son
Antique Carpets**
139 East 57th Street
New York, NY 10022
212-758-3900, 800-247-0001

Paris Ceramics
150 East 58th Street
New York, NY 10155
212-644-2784

Safavieh Carpets *
238 East 59th Street
New York, NY 10022
212-888-7847

Stark Carpet *
979 Third Avenue
New York, NY 10022
212-752-9000

V'Soske *
155 East 56th Street
New York, NY 10022
212-688-1150

Furniture

ABC Carpet & Home
888 Broadway
New York, NY 10003
212-473-3000

Agostino Antiques
808 Broadway
New York, NY 10003
212-533-3355

Alan Moss
436 Lafayette Street
New York, NY 10003
212-473-1310

Amy Perlin Antiques
1020 Lexington Avenue
New York, NY 10021
212-744-4923

Ann-Morris Antiques
239 East 60th Street
New York, NY 10022
212-755-3308

Furniture

Anthony Victoria
By appointment only
212-755-2549

Charles Pollack Reproductions
through Watkins & Fonthill *
979 Third Avenue
New York, NY 10022
212-755-6700

David Duncan Antiques
227 East 60th Street
New York, NY 10022
212-688-0666

David Stutmann
192 6th Avenue
New York, NY 10013
212-226-5717

DeLorenzo Gallery
958 Madison Avenue
New York, NY 10021
212-249-7575

The Devon Shop
111 East 27th Street
New York, NY 10016
212-686-1760

Didier Aaron & Cie
32 East 67th Street
New York, NY 10021
212-988-5248

Far Eastern Antiques *
799 Broadway
New York, NY 10003
212-460-5030

Florian Papp Antiques
962 Madison Avenue
New York, NY 10021
212-288-6770

J. Garving Mecking
72 East 11th Street
New York, NY 10003
212-677-4316

Jonas Upholstery *
44 West 18th Street
New York, NY 10011
212-691-2777

Kentshire Galleries
37 East 12th Street
New York, NY 10003
212-673-6644

L'Art de Vivre
11 East 26th Street
New York, NY 10010
212-739-6205

Maison Gerard
53 East 10th Street
New York, NY 10003
212-674-7611

Michael Connors
39 Great Jones Street
New York, NY 10012
212-473-0377

Newel Art Galleries
425 East 53rd Street
New York, NY 10022
212-758-1970

Niall Smith Antiques
344 Bleeker Street
New York, NY 10014
212-255-0660

Philip Collek Ltd.
830 Broadway
New York, NY 10012
212-505-2300

Galerie Renee Antiques
8 East 12th Street
New York, NY 10003
212-929-6914

Reymer-Jourdan Antiques
43 East 10th Street
New York, NY 10003
212-674-4470

Robert Jackson
P.O. Box 117
Germantown, NY 12526

Rose Cumming *
979 Third Avenue
New York, NY 10022
212-593-2060

Sarah Latham-Kearns
By appointment only
212-505-9127

Lighting

Abat Jours Custom Lamp Shades *
232 East 59th Street
New York, New York 10022
212-753-5455

Alan Moss
436 Lafayette Street
New York, NY 10003
212-473-1310

Florence Sack Ltd.
621 Warren St.
Hudson, NY 12534
518-822-0363

Marvin Alexander
315 East 62nd Street
New York, NY 10021
212-838-2320

Objets Plus *
315 East 62nd Street
New York, NY 10021
212-832-3386

Retro Modern Studio
58 East 11th Street
2nd Floor
New York, NY 10003
212-674-0530

Stephen McKay Lighting Design
225 Lafayette Street
New York, NY 10012
212-966-3858

Vincent Mulford
711 Warren Street
Hudson, NY 12534
518-828-5489

Weinstein Galleries
793 Madison Avenue
New York, NY 10021
212-717-6333

Tile

Country Floors
15 East 16th Street
New York, NY 10001
212-627-8300

Walker & Zanger
31 Warren Place
Mount Vernon, NY 10550
914-667-1600

Workrooms

Maury Shor, Inc.
1056 Washington Ave.
Bronx, NY 10456
718-993-0200

Paint

Donald Kaufman Color
410 West 13th Street
New York, NY 10014
212-243-2766

* Through architects and designers

Bruce Bierman created an elegant closet and dressing area for his client.

NEW INTERNATIONAL
PAGES 52—77

Featured Designers and Architects

Bruce Bierman Design
29 West 15th Street
New York, NY 10011
212-242-3563, 212-243-1935

Donald McKay Studio
83 Alcina Avenue
Toronto, M6G 2E7 Canada
416-651-9002

John Keenen
Keenen/Riley
526 West 26th Street
New York, NY 10001
212-645-9210

Kerry Joyce Associates, Inc.
115 North La Brea Avenue
Los Angeles, CA 90036
323-938-4442

Ricardo Legoretta, Architect
Mexico City, Mexico
011-52-5-25-1-96-98

Sills Huniford Associates
30 East 67th Street
New York, NY 10021
212-988-1636

Thomas O'Brien
Aero Studios
132 Spring Street
New York, NY 10012
212-966-4700

Accessories

Aero
132 Spring Street
New York, NY 10012
212-966-1500

Banana Republic Home
888-BRSTYLE

Deco Deluxe
993 Lexington Avenue
New York, NY 10021
212-472-7222

Donghia
979 Third Avenue
New York, NY 10022
212-935-3713, 800-DONGHIA

Dwellings
800-95-DECOR

Historical Materialism
125 Crosby Street
New York, NY 10012
212-431-3424

Jeffrey Aronoff
16 West 23rd Street
3rd Floor
New York, NY 10010
212-645-3155

Jerry Solomon Enterprises
960 North La Brea Avenue
Los Angeles, CA 90038
323-851-7241

Jonathan Adler
465 Broome Street
New York, NY 10003
212-941-8950

J. Pocker & Son
135 East 63rd Street
New York, NY 10021
212-838-5488, 800-443-3116

Luxor Gallery
238 East 60th Street
New York, NY 10022
212-832-3633

Manuel Canovas *
through Cowtan & Tout
979 Third Avenue
New York, NY 10022
212-647-6900

Peter Roberts Antiques
134 Spring Street
New York, NY 10003
212-226-4777

Portico
139 Spring Street
New York, NY 10012
212-941-7722

Robert Altman
1148 Second Avenue
New York, NY 10021
212-832-3490

Takashimaya
693 Fifth Avenue
New York, NY 10022
212-350-0100, 800-565-6785

Troy
138 Greene Street
New York, NY 10012
212-941-4777

Fabrics, Wall Coverings, Trims

Caldelle Leather
1649 12th Street
Santa Monica, CA 90404
310-314-8800

Clarence House *
211 East 58th Street
New York, NY 10022
212-752-2890, 800-632-0076

Cortina Leather
5 West 20th Street
New York, NY 10011
212-463-0645

Donghia
979 Third Avenue
New York, NY 10022
212-935-3713, 800-DONGHIA

Gretchen Bellinger *
31 Ontario Street
P.O. Box 64
Cohoes, NY 12047
518-235-2828

J. Robert Scott *
979 Third Avenue
New York, NY 10022
212-755-4910

Larsen *
through Cowtan & Tout
979 Third Avenue
New York, NY 10022
212-647-6900

Manuel Canovas *
through Cowtan & Tout
979 Third Avenue
New York, NY 10022
212-647-6900

Fabrics, Wall Coverings, Trims

Pierre Frey *
12 East 33rd Street
New York, NY 10022
212-213-3099

Rogers & Goffigon *
979 Third Avenue
New York, NY 10022
212-888-3242

Zimmer & Rohde *
979 Third Avenue
New York, NY 10022
212-758-5357

Flooring

A. Morjikian Co. Inc. *
979 Third Avenue
New York, NY 10022
212-753-8695

Entree Libre
110 Wooster Street
New York, NY 10012
212-431-5279

Gucci Home Collection
800-388-6785

Hokanson *
979 Third Avenue
New York, NY 10022
212-758-0669, 800-243-7771

Patterson, Flynn & Martin *
979 Third Avenue
New York, NY 10022
212-688-7700

Safavieh Carpets *
238 East 59th Street
New York, NY 10022
212-888-7847

Furniture

Aero
132 Spring Street
New York, NY 10012
212-966-1500

Barry Friedman Ltd.
32 East 67th Street
New York, NY 10021
212-794-8950

Capitol Furnishings
259 Elizabeth Street
New York, NY 10012
212-925-6760

Carol Gratale *
979 Third Avenue
New York, NY 10022
212-838-8670

Christian Liaigre at Holly Hunt *
1844 Merchandise Mart
Chicago, IL 60654
312-661-1900

Classic Sofa
5 West 22nd Street
New York, NY 10010
212-620-0485

Coconut Company
131 Greene Street
New York, NY 10012
212-539-1940

Dakota Jackson *
979 Third Avenue
New York, NY 10022
212-838-9444

David Stypmann
190 Avenue of the Americas
New York, NY 10013
212-226-5717

DeLorenzo
958 Madison Avenue
New York, NY 10021
212-249-7575

Dennis Miller Associates
306 East 61st Street
New York, NY 10021
212-355-4550

Donghia *
979 Third Avenue
New York, NY 10022
212-935-3713, 800-DONGHIA

Gueridon
359 Lafayette Street
New York, NY 10012
212-677-7740

IL Euro
45 Greene Street
New York, NY 10013
212-625-1494

Interieurs
149 Franklin Street
New York, NY 10013
212-343-0800

James Jennings Furniture *
8471 Melrose Avenue
West Hollywood, CA 90069
323-655-7823

Jonas Upholstery *
44 West 18th Street
10th Floor
New York, NY 10011
212-691-2777

JM Upholstery *
10-10 44th Avenue
Long Island City, NY 11101
718-786-0104

JWA Furniture *
74 Guernsey Street
Brooklyn, NY 11222
718-599-9828

Karl Kemp & Associates
29 East 11th Street
New York, NY 10003
212-254-1877

Knoll *
105 Wooster Street
New York, NY 10012
212-343-4000

L'Art de Vivre
11 East 26th Street
New York, NY 10010
212-739-6205

Louis Bofferding
by appointment only
212-744-6725

Maison Gerard Ltd.
53 East 10th Street
New York, NY 10003
212-674-7611

Mattaliano
205 West Wacker Drive
Chicago, IL 60606
312-853-9444

Palazzetti
515 Madison Avenue
New York, NY 10022
212-832-1199, 888-881-1199

Peter-Roberts Antiques
134 Spring Street
New York, NY 10003
212-226-4777

Pucci International *
44 West 18th Street
New York, NY 10011
212-633-0452

Salon Moderne
281 Lafayette Street
New York, NY 10012
212-219-3439

Shelter
1433 Fifth Street
Santa Monica, CA 90401
310-451-3536

Sonrisa
22 West 21st Street
New York, NY 10010
212-627-7474

The Terence Conran Shop
407 East 59th Street
New York, NY 10022
212-755-9079

Todd Hase Furniture Inc.
51 Wooster Street
New York, NY 10013
212-334-3568

Wyeth
151 Franklin Street
New York, NY 10013
212-925-5278

* Through architects and designers

Lighting

Aero
132 Spring Street
New York, NY 10012
212-966-1500

Cedric Hartman *
979 Third Avenue
New York, NY 10022
212-421-8755, 800-423-3742

Donghia *
979 Third Avenue
New York, NY 10022
212-935-3713, 800-DONGHIA

George Kovacs
67-25 Otto Road
Glendale, NY 11385
718-628-5201

Maxfield
8825 Melrose Avenue
Los Angeles, CA 90069
310-274-8800

Robert Gingold Antiques
95 East 10th Street
New York, NY 10003
212-475-4008

Jacques Grange and his clients delight in the mix of rustic and refined.

COUNTRY LUXE
PAGES 78–105

Featured Architects and Designers

Bennett & Judie Weinstock Interiors, Inc.
2026 Delancey Place
Philadelphia, PA 19103
215-735-2026

Jacques Grange
118 rue du Fauborg Saint-Honoré
75008 Paris, France
33-1-47-42-47-34

Joanne Hudson Associates
2400 Market Street
Philadelphia, PA 19103
215-568-5501

John Barman Interior Design
500 Park Avenue, Suite 21A
New York, NY 10022
212-838-3453

J. Doyle Design
36 West 20th Street
8th Floor
New York, NY 10003
212-533-5455

Diamond Baratta
270 Lafayette Street
New York, NY 10003
212-966-8892

Accessories

French General
35 Crosby Street
New York, NY 10003
212-343-7474

Le Fanion
299 West 4th Street
New York, NY 10011
212-463-8760

Malmaison Antiques, New York
253 East 74th Street
New York, NY 10021
212-288-7569

Willet Stained Glass Studios, Inc.
10 East Moreland Avenue
Philadelphia, PA 19118
215-247-5721

Bathroom, Kitchen

P.E. Guerin
23 Jane Street
New York, NY 10014
212-243-5270

Restoration Hardware
800-762-1005

Sherle Wagner International
60 East 57th Street
New York, NY 10022
212-758-3300, 888-9WAGNER

Sub-Zero
800-444-7820

Waterworks
800-899-6757

Wm. Ohs Inc.
5095 Peoria Street
Denver, CO 80239
303-371-6550

Fabrics, Wall Coverings, Trims

Bennison Fabrics *
76 Greene Street
New York, NY 10003
212-941-1212

Brunschwig & Fils *
979 Third Avenue
New York, NY 10022
212-838-7878

Christopher Hyland *
979 Third Avenue
New York, NY 10022
212-688-6121

Clarence House *
211 East 58th Street
New York, NY 10022
212-752-2890, 800-632-0076

* Through architects and designers

Fabrics, Wall Coverings, Trims

Cowtan & Tout *
979 Third Avenue
New York, NY 10022
212-647-6900

Etro USA Inc. *
979 Third Avenue
New York, NY 10022
212-755-6700

Old World Weavers *
979 Third Avenue
New York, NY 10022
212-355-7186

Paula Rubenstein
65 Prince Street
New York, NY 10003
212-966-8954

Pierre Frey *
979 Third Avenue
New York, NY 10022
212-935-3713

Robert Allen *
979 Third Avenue
New York, NY 10022
212-421-1200

Scalamandre *
942 Third Avenue
New York, NY 10022
212-980-3888, 800-932-4361

Schumacher *
800-332-3384

Flooring

Elizabeth Eakins Inc.
21 East 65th Street
New York, NY 10021
212-628-1950

Hunters & Collectors
Bridgehampton, NY
516-537-4233

Stark Carpet *
979 Third Avenue
New York, NY 10022
212-752-9000

Furniture

ABC Carpet & Home
888 Broadway
New York, NY 10010
212-473-3000

Anthropologie
375 West Broadway
New York, NY 10012
212-343-7070, 800-753-2038

Avery on Bond
2 Bond Street
New York, NY 10012
212-614-1492

Church Street Trading
4 Railroad Street
Great Barrington, MA 01230
413-528-6120

Classic Heirlooms
1505 Thermal Avenue
San Diego, CA 92154
619-429-6288

Coming to America
276 Lafayette Street
New York, NY 10012
212-343-2968

DeAngelis, Inc. *
312 East 95th Street
New York, NY 10128
212-348-8225

Elaine Rush Antiques
at Barnum Interiors
965 South Main Street
Great Barrington, MA 01230
413-528-0812

Gray Gardens
461 Broome Street
New York, NY 10013
212-966-7116

Keystone
746 Warren Street
Hudson, NY 12534
518-822-1019

McKenzie-Childs
940 Madison Avenue
New York, NY 10021
888-665-1999

Pottery Barn
800-922-5507

Ruby Beets Antiques
Bridgehampton, NY
516-966-7116

The Rural Collection
117 Perry Street
New York, NY 10014
212-645-4488

Shabby Chic
93 Greene Street
New York, NY 10003
212-274-9842

Susan Parrish
390 Bleeker Street
New York, NY 10014
212-645-5020

The Yard Couple
Sag Harbor, NY
516-725-7200

Lighting

ABC Carpet & Home
888 Broadway
New York, NY 10010
212-473-3000

Ann-Morris Antiques
239 East 60th Street
New York, NY 10022
212-755-3308

Anthropologie
800-753-2038

Joseph Richter Light Fixtures
249 East 57th Street
New York, NY 10022
212-755-6094

Van Parys Studio
205 Pennsylvania Avenue
Fortescue, NJ 08234
609-447-3067

Tile

Amsterdam Corporation
150 East 58th Street
New York, NY 10155
212-644-1350

Artistic Tile, Inc.
79 Fifth Avenue
New York, NY 10003
212-727-9331

Country Floors
15 East 16th Street
New York, NY 10003
212-627-8300

Workrooms

Meg Shay Studio, Inc.
1018 Merion Sq. Road
Gladwyne, PA 19035
610-896-2191

Building Materials

Fypon Inc.
800-537-5349

* Through architects and designers

Jennifer Post designs classic, light-filled modern interiors enlivened by splashes of strong color.

MINIMALISM
PAGES 106–133

Featured Architects and Designers

Jennifer Post Interior Design
25 East 67th Street, 8D
New York, NY 10021
212-734-7994

Mark Demsky Architects, Ltd.
1963 North Halsted Street
Chicago, IL 60614
312-280-5300

Gabellini Associates Architects
665 Broadway
New York, NY 10010
212-388-1700

Niedermaier, Inc.
2650 West Fulton Street
Chicago, IL 60612
773-722-1000, 800-260-8123

Accessories

Asiaphile
606 North Larchmont Boulevard
Suite 4D
Los Angeles, CA 90004
213-856-9838

B&B Gallery
601 West 26th Street
14th Floor
New York, NY 10001
212-243-0840

Calvin Klein Home
800-294-7978

* Through architects and designers

Furniture Company
818 Greenwich Street
New York, NY 10014
212-352-2010

H
335 East 9th Street
New York, NY 10003
212-477-2631

Interieurs
149 Franklin Street
New York, NY 10013
212-343-0800

Jacques Carcanagues
106 Spring Street
New York, NY 10012
212-925-8110

MoMA Design Store
44 West 53rd Street
New York, NY 10019
212-767-1050, 800-447-6662

Moss
146 Greene Street
New York, NY 10012
212-226-2190

Mxyplyzyk
125 Greenwich Avenue
New York, NY 10014
212-989-4300

Property, NY
14 Wooster Street
New York, NY 10013
917-237-0123

Shi
233 Elizabeth Street
New York, NY 10012
212-334-4300

Ted Muehling
47 Greene Street
New York, NY 10013
212-431-3825

William Lipton Ltd
27 East 61st Street
New York, NY 10021
212-751-8131

Bath, Kitchen

Ad Hoc Softwares
136 Wooster Street
New York, NY 10012
212-982-7703

Bellora
123 West 20th Street
New York, NY 10011
212-929-7574

Barber Wilson & Co. Ltd.
through SoHo Corp
800-969-SOHO

Bisazza
175 Fifth Avenue
Suite 2300
New York, NY 10010
212-888-1794

Boffi SoHo
31½ Greene Street
New York, NY 10013
212-431-8282

Bulthaup
578 Broadway
Suite 306
New York, NY 10012
212-966-7183

Cherry Creek/Vitraform
3500 Blake Street
Denver, CO 80205
303-295-1010, 800-338-5725

Czech & Speake
through Waterworks
800-899-6757

Hastings Tile & Bath
230 Park Avenue South
New York, NY 10010
212-674-9700

Ikea
800-434-IKEA

Kroin
800-OK-KROIN

Nemo Tile
48 East 21st Street
New York, NY 10010
212-505-0009

Siematic
800-765-5266

Valcucine
152 Wooster Street
New York, NY 10003
212-253-5969

Fabrics, Wall Coverings, Trims

Henry Calvin *
979 Third Avenue
New York, NY 10022
212-935-3713

Joseph Noble *
979 Third Avenue
New York, NY 10022
212-421-8755

Kirk Brummel *
979 Third Avenue
New York, NY 10022
212-477-8590

Kravet Fabrics Inc. *
979 Third Avenue
New York, NY 10022
212-421-6363, 800-645-9068

Manuel Canovas *
through Cowtan & Tout
979 Third Avenue
New York, NY 10022
212-647-6900

Nuno *
979 Third Avenue
New York, NY 10022
212-421-9114

Pollack & Associates *
979 Third Avenue
New York, NY 10022
212-421-8755

Flooring

Einstein Moomjy
150 East 58th Street
New York, NY 10155
212-758-0900

Larsen *
through Cowtan & Tout
979 Third Avenue
New York, NY 10022
212-647-6900

Lamontage
210 11th Avenue
New York, NY 10001
212-989-2732

* Through architects and designers

Odegard
200 Lexington Avenue
New York, NY 10016
212-545-0069, 800-670-8836

Furniture

American Wing Antiques
2415 Main Street
Bridgehampton, NY 11932
516-537-3319

Antiques On Lyme
18 Lyme Street
Old Lyme, CT 06371
860-434-3901

Art & Industrial Design
399 Lafayette Street
New York, NY 10003
212-477-0116

B&B Italia *
150 East 58th Street
New York, NY 10155
212-758-4046, 800-872-1697

Balasses House
208 Main Street
Amagansett, NY 11930
516-267-3032

Barlow Tyrie Inc.
1263 Glen Avenue
Moorestown, NJ 08057
800-451-7467

Black Whale Antiques
5 Town Street
Hadlyme, CT 06439
860-526-5073

Brown Jordan
9860 Gridley Street
El Monte, CA 91731
626-443-8971

Campaniello Enterprises, Inc.
225 East 57th Street
New York, NY 10022
212-371-3700

Cappellini Modern Age
102 Wooster Street
New York, NY 10003
212-966-0069

Cassina
155 East 56th Street
New York, NY 10022
212-245-2121

Christian Liaigre at Holly Hunt *
1844 Merchandise Mart
Chicago, IL 60654
312-661-1900

DKNY
655 Madison Avenue
New York, NY 10023
212-223-3569

Donzella
17 White Street
New York, NY 10013
212-965-8919

Format
12 West 57th Street
New York, NY 10019
212-582-7170

Furniture Company
818 Greenwich Street
New York, NY 10014
212-352-2010

George Nakashima Woodworkers
1847 Aquetong Road
New Hope, PA 18938
215-862-2272

Global Table
107 Sullivan Street
New York, NY 10012
212-431-5839

Herman Miller *
855 East Main Avenue
Zeeland, MI 49464
616-654-3000, 800-851-1196

Hugues Chevalier through Studium V *
150 East 58th Street
New York, NY 10155
212-486-1811

ICF Group *
704 Executive Bldg.
Valley Cottage, NY 10989
914-268-0700, 800-426-6471

James Jennings Furniture *
8471 Melrose Avenue
West Hollywood, CA 90069
323-655-7823

James Mont through Liz O'Brien
41 Wooster Street
New York, NY 10003
212-343-0935

Kartell
45 Greene Street
New York, NY 10013
212-966-6665

Kneedler Faucher *
8687 Melrose Avenue
Los Angeles, CA 90069
310-855-1313

Knoll *
105 Wooster Street
New York, NY 10003
212-434-4000

La Mode Upholstery Co.*
3280 Broadway
New York, NY 10027
212-862-3220

Ligne Roset
1090 Third Avenue
New York, NY 10021
212-794-2903

Limn
290 Townsend Street
San Francisco, CA 94107
415-543-5466

Luminaire
301 West Superior Street
Chicago, IL 60610
312-664-9582, 800-494-4358

Neidermaier, Inc.
2650 West Fulton Street
Chicago, IL 60612
773-722-1000, 800-260-8123

Furniture

Nicole Farhi
14 East 60th Street
New York, NY 10021
212-421-7720

Palumbo
972 Lexington Avenue
New York, NY 10022
212-734-7630

Poliform *
150 East 58th Street
New York, NY 10155
212-421-1220, 888-POLIFORM

Richard Schultz Design
806 Gravel Pike
Palm, PA 18070
215-679-2222

Troy
138 Greene Street
New York, NY 10012
212-941-4777

Victor Weinblatt Antiques
P.O. Box 335
South Hadley, MA 01075
413-538-7773

Vitra *
149 Fifth Avenue
New York, NY 10010
212-539-1900, 800-338-4872

Waldo's Designs
620 Almont Dr.
Los Angeles, CA 90069
310-278-1803

Lighting

Akari Associates
32-37 Vernon Boulevard
Long Island City, NY 11106
718-721-2308

Ann-Morris Antiques
239 East 60th Street
New York, NY 10022
212-755-3308

Artemide
46 Greene Street
New York, NY 10013
212-925-1588

Flos USA
through Cassina
155 East 56th Street
New York, NY 10022
212-245-2121

Grand Brass Lamp Parts, Inc.
221 Grand Street
New York, NY 10013
212-226-2567

Ingo Maurer
89 Grand Street
New York, NY 10013
212-965-8817

Just Shades
21 Spring Street
New York, NY 10012
212-966-2757

Leucos
11 Mayfield Avenue
P.O. Box 7829
Edison, NJ 08818-7829
732-225-0010, 800-832-3360

Luceplan
315 Hudson Street
New York, NY 10013
212-989-6265, 800-268-7790

Workrooms

H.P. Broom-Housewright
162 Ferry Road
Hadlyme, CT 06439
860-526-9836

Jon Gellman Designs
314 Seventh Street
Jersey City, NJ 07302
201-418-8707

Lorraine Kirke's kitchen has ample space to store her many favorite things.

BOHEMIAN CHIC
PAGES 134–161

Featured Architects and Designers

Story
4 Wilkes Street
Spitalfields, London
E16 QSF
England
011-44-207-377-0313

Cicognani Kalla Architects
16 East 53rd Street
New York, NY 10022
212-308-4811

Albert, Righter & Tittmann
58 Winter Street
Boston, MA 02108
617-451-5740

Accessories

BoHo Co.
91 Crosby Street
New York, NY 10012
212-4331-4304

Gray Gardens
461 Broome Street
New York, NY 10003
212-966-7116

Marguerite Lorchard Designs
174 Thompson Street
New York, NY 10012
212-598-5161

Ruby Beets Antiques
Bridgehampton, NY
516-537-2802

* Through architects and designers

Accessories

Sarajo
130 Greene Street
New York, NY 10012
212-966-6156

Sinotique
19-A Mott Street
New York, NY 10013
212-587-2393

Stone Road
328 Montauk Highway
Wainscott, NY 11975
516-537-5656

Tink
42 Rivington Street
New York, NY 10002
212-529-6356

Tucker Robbins
366 West 15th Street
New York, NY 10011
212-366-4427

Fabrics, Wall Coverings, Trims

Casita
48 East 12th Street
New York, NY 10003
212-253-1925

Cora Ginsberg
by appointment only
212-744-1352

Françoise Nunnalle
by appointment only
212-246-4281

MeiLiu Dong
40 West 25th Street
New York, NY 10001
718-520-0042

Sanderson & Company *
979 Third Avenue
New York, NY 10022
212-319-7222

Sarajo
130 Greene Street
New York, NY 10012
212-966-6156

Symourgh International
34 East 34th Street
New York, NY 10016
212-688-3756

Tucker Robbins
366 West 15th Street
New York, NY 10011
212-366-4427

Flooring

Forbo Industries
P.O. Box 667
Humboldt Industrial Park
Hazelton, PA 18201
570-459-0771, 800-842-7839

Hunters & Collectors
Bridgehampton, NY
516-537-4233

The Silk Trading Co.
(J. Mabley Fabric Co.)
39 North Moore Street
New York, NY 10013
212-966-5464

Mark Shilen Gallery
109 Greene Street
New York, NY 10012
212-925-3394

Symourgh International
34 East 34th Street
New York, NY 10016
212-688-3756

Furniture

ABC Carpet & Home
888 Broadway
New York, NY 10003
212-473-3000

Arts du Monde
154 Spring Street
New York, NY 10012
212-226-3702

Asian Arts, Moke Mokotoff
257 West 17th Street
New York, NY 10011
212-741-4443

Craft Caravan Inc.
63 Greene Street
New York, NY 10012
212-431-6669

George Smith Sofas & Chairs
73 Spring Street
New York, NY 10012
212-226-4747

Jacques Carcanagues
106 Spring Street
New York, New York 10012
212-925-8110

Jamson-Whyte Inc.
47 Wooster Street
New York, NY 10003
212-965-9405

J.H. Antiques
174 Duane Street
New York, NY 10013
212-965-1443

MeiLiu Dong
40 West 25th Street
New York, NY 10001
718-520-0042

Pottery Barn
800-922-5507

Ruby Beets
Bridgehampton, NY
516-537-2802

The Rural Collection
117 Perry Street
New York, NY 10014
212-645-4488

Secondhand Rose
138 Duane Street
New York, NY 10013
212-393-9002

Tucker Robbins
366 West 15th Street, 5th Floor
New York, NY 10011
212-366-4427

The Yard Couple
Sag Harbor, NY
516-725-7200

Lighting

BoHo Co.
91 Crosby Street
New York, NY 10012
212-431-4304

Le Fanion
229 West 4th Street
New York, NY 10014
212-463-8760

Potted Gardens Ltd.
27 Bedford Street
New York, NY 10014
212-255-4797

Urban Archaeology
285 Lafayette Street
New York, NY 10012
212-431-4646

Sarajo
130 Greene Street
New York, NY 10012
212-966-6156

Stephanie Odegard *
200 Lexington Avenue
New York, NY 10016
212-545-0069

Walzworkinc.
20 West 20th Street
New York New York 10011
212-229-2299

Tile

American Rag
150 South La Brea Avenue
Los Angeles, CA 90036
323-935-3154

Clair Soleil
Design Center of the Americas
1855 Griffin Road
Dania, FL 33004
954-929-0181

* Through architects and designers

Workrooms

Jean François Aime
C. Blaichman Construction
311 East 18th Street
New York, NY 10003
212-505-5270

Secondhand Rose
138 Duane Street
New York, NY 10013
212-393-9002

Studio 40
40 Great Jones Street
New York, NY 10012
212-420-8631

Tribeca Upholstery
103 Reade Street
New York, NY 10013
212-349-3010

Vahakn Arslanian
212-463-7327

Gauzere's treasures include a
ruby turtle and the Duchesse de
Berry's embroidered portfolio.

GRAND TOUR
PAGES 162–189

Featured Architects and Designers

Quadrille Wallpapers and Fabrics *
979 Third Avenue
New York, NY 10022
212-753-2995

Lars Bolander Design Inc.
375 South County Road
Palm Beach, FL 33480
561-832-5108

Patrick Naggar and Terese Carpenter
Nile Inc.
38 East 64th Street
New York, NY 10021
212-688-8860

Accessories

Ariadne Galleries
970 Madison Avenue
New York, NY 10021
212-772-3388

Ben Wilson Antiques
Hudson, NY
510-822-0866

Bob Pryor Antiques
1023 Lexington Avenue
New York, NY 10021
212-688-1516

Dimson Homma
20 East 67th Street
New York, NY 10021
212-439-7950

The Drawing Room of Newport
152 Spring Street
Newport, RI 02840
401-841-5060

H.M. Luther Antiques
61 East 11th Street
New York, NY 10003
212-505-1485

Pamela Walker
by appointment only
212-288-0370

Treasures & Trifles
409 Bleeker Street
New York, NY 10014
212-243-2723

Fabrics, Wall Coverings, Trims

Bergamo *
979 Third Avenue
New York, NY 10022
212-888-3333

Brunschwig & Fils *
979 Third Avenue
New York, NY 10022
212-838-7878

Chelsea Editions *
232 East 59th Street
6th Floor
New York, NY 10022
212-758-0005

Clarence House*
211 East 58th Street
New York, NY 10022
212-752-2890, 800-632-0076

Fonthill *
979 Third Avenue
New York, NY 10022
212-755-6700

Haas Fabrics *
979 Third Avenue
New York, NY 10022
212-753-2995

Quadrille Wallpapers and Fabrics, Inc. *
979 Third Avenue
New York, NY 10022
212-753-2995

Rogers & Goffigon *
979 Third Avenue
New York, NY 10022
212-888-3242

Fittings, Fixtures

P.E. Guerin
23 Jane Street
New York, NY 10014
212-243-5270

* Through architects and designers

Flooring

Carpet Innovations
588 Broadway
New York, NY 10013
212966-9445

Stark Carpet *
979 Third Avenue
New York, NY 10022
212-752-9000

Furniture

Arenskjold Antiques Art
Hudson, NY
518-828-2800

Bernd Goeckler Antiques
30 East 10th Street
New York, NY 10003
212-777-9209

Burden & Izett Ltd.
180 Duane Street
New York, NY 10013
212-941-8247

David L. Petrovsky Ltd., Antiques
Hudson, NY
518-822-0866

Florentine Craftsmen
46-24 28th Street
Long Island City, NY 11101
718-937-7632

Hadassah Antiques
1050 Second Avenue, Gallery 75
New York, NY 10022
212-751-0009

H.M. Luther Antiques
61 East 11th Street
New York, NY 10003
212-505-1485

Les Deus Iles
104 West 27th Street
12th Floor
New York, NY 10001
212-604-9437

Pagoda Antiques
Hudson, NY
518-822-1025

Ramson House
32 Franklin Street
New Port, RI 02840
401-847-0555

Remains
130 West 28th Street
New York, NY 10001
212-675-8051

Reymer-Jourdan Antiques
29 East 10th Street
New York, NY 10003
212-674-4470

Ritter-Antik, Inc.
35 East 10th Street
New York, NY 10003
212-673-2213

Svenska Mobler
154 North La Brea Avenue
Los Angeles, CA 90036
323-934-4452

Turbulence
812 Broadway
New York, NY 10003
212-598-9030

Yale R. Burge Antiques
315 East 62nd Street
New York, NY 10021
212-838-4005

Lighting

George N. Antiques
67 East 11th Street
New York, NY 10003
212-505-5599

Stephanie Odegard *
200 Lexington Avenue
New York, NY 10016
212-545-0069

Stillwaggon Antiques
Hudson, NY
518-828-2039

* Through architects and designers

Garouste & Bonetti chairs
complement the table
Martin Szekely designed
for a French interior.

MID-CENTURY MODERN
PAGES 190–223

Featured Architects and Designers

George Nakashima Woodworker S.A.
1847 Aquetong Road
New Hope, PA 18938
215-862-2272

Garouste & Bonetti
1 rue Oberkampf
Paris 75011
France
011-33-1-48-05-8651

William Stewart Designs Inc.
349 Peachtree Hills Avenue, N.E.,
Suite C2B
Atlanta, GA 30305
404-816-2501

Accessories

Chilewich
7 East 30th Street
New York, NY 10016
212-679-9204

Dom
382 West Broadway
New York, NY 10012
212-334-5580

Frank Lloyd Wright Preservation Trust
951 Chicago Avenue
Oak Park, IL 60302-2097
708-848-1606, 877-848-3559

Michael Anchin Glass Co.
245 Elizabeth Street
New York, NY 10012
212-925-1470

Moss
146 Greene Street
New York, NY 10012
212-226-2190

Nambe
1127 Siler road
Santa Fe, NM 87505
505-471-2912

The Orange Chicken
146 Reade Street
New York, NY 10013
212-431-0337

Zao
175 Orchard Street
New York, NY 10002
212-505-0500

Fabrics, Wallcoverings, Trims

Osborne & Little *
979 Third Avenue
New York, NY 10022
212-751-3333

Flooring

Designer Carpets, Inc. *
800-241-0456

Furniture

1950
440 Lafayette Street
New York, NY 10003
212-995-1950

20th Century Antiques
1044 North Highland
Virginia Highlands
Atlanta, GA 30306
404-892-2065

280 Modern
280 Lafayette Street
New York, NY 10012
212-941-5825

Alan Moss
436 Lafayette Street
New York, NY 10003
212-473-1310

Antik
104 Franklin Street
New York, NY 10013
212-343-0471

Area...ID
262 Elizabeth Street
New York, NY 10012
212-219-9903

Art and Industrial Design
399 Lafayette Street
New York, NY 10003
212-477-0116

Auto
805 Washington Street
New York, NY 10014
212-229-2292

Bertoi
324 East 9th Street
New York, NY 10003
212-614-8742

Breukelen
68 Gansevoort Street
New York, NY 10014
212-645-2216

Cappellini Modern Age
102 Wooster Street
New York, NY 10012
212-966-0669

Carlos Alves
Miami Beach, FL
305-673-3824

Carpe Diem
187 Sixth Avenue
New York, NY 10013
212-337-0018

Cassina
155 East 56th Street
New York, NY 10022
212-245-2121

City Barn Antiques
269 Lafayette Street
New York, NY 10003
212-941-5757

* Through architects and designers

Furniture

Collage 20th Century Classics
2820 North Henderson
Dallas, TX 75206
214-828-9888

David Rago Auction
333 North Main Street
Lambertville, NJ 08530-1512
609-397-9374

De Vera
29 Maiden Lane
San Francisco, CA 94108
415-788-0828

Domus, Inc. *
800-432-2713

Donzella
17 White Street
New York, NY 10013
212-965-8919

The End of History
548½ Hudson Street
New York, NY 10014
212-647-7598

Fat Chance
162 North La Brea Avenue
Los Angeles, CA 90036
323-930-1960

Form and Function
95 Vandam Street
New York, NY 10013
212-414-1800

Gallerie du Beyrie
393 West Broadway, 3rd Floor
New York, NY 10013
212-219-9565

Gansevoort Gallery
72 Gansevoort Street
New York, NY 10014
212-633-0555

Cap Sud
50 Bond Street
New York, NY 10012
212-260-9114

Gaston
125 Grand Street
New York, NY 10003
212-219-3846

George Nakashima Woodworker
1847 Aquetong Road
New Hope, PA 18938
215-862-2272

H55
17 Little West 12th Street
New York, NY 10014
212-462-4559

Herman Miller for the Home
800-646-4400

Hirschl & Adler
21 East 70th Street
New York, NY 10021
212-535-8810

Kartell
45 Greene Street
New York, NY 10013
212-966-6665

Knoll *
105 Wooster Street
New York, NY 10012
212-343-4000

Kenyon Studios
9205 West Van Buren Street
Tolleson, AZ 85353
623-936-8066

Lin-Weinberg
84 Wooster Street
New York, NY 10012
212-219-3022

Lisbeth & Co.
259 Elizabeth Street
New York, NY 10012
212-966-9559

Lobel Modern
207 West 18th Street
New York, Ny 10011
212-242-9075

Lost City Arts
275 Lafayette Street
New York, NY 10012
212-941-8025

Modern Living
8775 Beverly Boulevard
Los Angeles, CA 90048
310-657-8775

Modernica
57 Greene Street
New York, NY 10012
212-219-1303

Mood Indigo
181 Prince Street
New York, NY 10012
212-254-1176

Neotu
545 West 34th Street
New York, NY 10001
212-695-9404

Phillip Northman
Cache Antiques & Flea Market
1845 Cheshire Bridge Road
Atlanta, GA 30324
404-815-0880

Gaetano Pesce
543 Broadway
Suite 5
New York, NY 10012
212-941-0280

Property
14 Wooster Street
New York, NY 10013
917-237-0123

R 20th Century Design
82 Franklin Street
New York, NY 10013
212-343-7979

reGeneration
38 Renwick Street
New York, NY 10003
212-741-2102

Robert Aibel Moderne Gallery
111 North Third Street
Philadelphia, PA 19106
215-923-8536

SEE, Ltd
920 Broadway
New York, NY 10010
212-228-3600

Totem Design Group
71 Franklin Street
New York, NY 10013
212-925-5506

White Furniture
85 White Street
New York, NY 10013
212-964-4694

Tile

Dal Tile
800-933-8453

Walker & Zanger
31 Warren Place
Mount Vernon, NY 10550
914-667-1600

* Through architects and designers

CREDITS

INTRODUCTION

PAGE 6, MICHEL ARNAUD; PAGE 8, PASCAL CHEVALLIER; PAGE 9, TOP, LAURIE LAMBRECHT
PAGE 9, BOTTOM, FERNANDO BENGOECHEA; PAGE 10, TOP, MATT HRANEK; PAGE 10, BOTTOM, ERIC BOMAN; PAGE 11, ANITA CALERO

UPDATED CLASSICS

PAGE 12, MELANIE ACEVEDO; PAGES 14–19, MICHAEL MUNDY; PAGES 20–25, MELANIE ACEVEDO; PAGES 26–31, MICHEL ARNAUD
PAGES 32–37, MELANIE ACEVEDO; PAGES 38–43, FERNANDO BENGOECHEA; PAGES 44–51, MELANIE ACEVEDO

NEW INTERNATIONAL

PAGE 52, TODD EBERLE; PAGES 54–59, ROBERT POLIDORI
PAGES 60–65, ANTOINE BOOTZ; PAGES 66–71, TODD EBERLE; PAGES 72–77, TODD EBERLE

COUNTRY LUXE

PAGE 78, LAURIE LAMBRECHT; PAGES 80–85, MICHEL ARNAUD
PAGES 86–93, HENRY BOURNE; PAGES 94–99, PIETER ESTERSOHN; PAGES 100–105, LAURIE LAMBRECHT

MINIMALISM

PAGE 106–115, TODD EBERLE; PAGES 116–121, ANITA CALERO
PAGES 122–127, WILLIAM ABRANOWICZ; PAGES 128–133, ANTOINE BOOTZ

BOHEMAIN CHIC

PAGE134–141, FRANÇOIS HALARD; PAGES 142–145, MELANIE ACEVEDO
PAGES 146–153, ERIC BOMAN; PAGES 154–161, MELANIE ACEVEDO

GRAND TOUR

PAGE 162, DANA GALLAGHER; PAGES 164–169, PASCAL CHEVALLIER
PAGES 170–175, ERIC BOMAN; PAGES 176–183, DANA GALLAGHER; PAGES 184–189, MELANIE ACEVEDO

MID-CENTURY MODERN

PAGE 190, FRANÇOIS DISCHINGER; PAGES 192–197, MICHEL ARNAUD; PAGES 198–203, FRANÇOIS DISCHINGER
PAGES 204–209,MICHAEL MUNDY; PAGES 210–213, FRANÇOIS DISCHINGER; PAGES 214–223, ALEXANDRE BAILHACHE

RESOURCES

PAGE 224,MELANIE ACEVEDO;PAGE 228, ANTOINE BOOTZ; PAGE 230, HENRY BOURNE; PAGE 232, ANTOINE BOOTZ
PAGE 234,MELANIE ACEVEDO; PAGE 234, PASCAL CHEVALLIER; PAGE 238, ALEXANDRE BAILHACHE.